CRAFTING A COLORFUL HOME

CRAFTING

A

COLORFUL

HOME

A ROOM-BY-ROOM GUIDE
TO PERSONALIZING YOUR
SPACE WITH COLOR

KRISTIN NICHOLAS

PHOTOGRAPHS BY RIKKI SNYDER

ROOST BOOKS

BOSTON & LONDON
2015

Roost Books
An imprint of Shambhala Publications, Inc.
Horticultural Hall
300 Massachusetts Avenue
Boston, Massachusetts 02115
roostbooks.com

Text and illustrations © 2015 by
Kristin Nicholas
Photographs © 2015 by Rikki Snyder

9 8 7 6 5 4 3 2 1

First Edition
Printed in China

♾ This edition is printed on acid-free
paper that meets the American National
Standards Institute Z39.48 Standard.
♻ Shambhala Publications makes every
effort to print on recycled paper.
For more information please visit
www.shambhala.com.

Distributed in the United States by Penguin
Random House LLC and in Canada by
Random House of Canada Ltd

BOOK DESIGN BY SHUBHANI SARKAR

Library of Congress Cataloging-in-
Publication Data

Nicholas, Kristin.
Crafting a colorful home: a room-by-room
guide to personalizing your space with color /
Kristin Nicholas; photographs by Rikki
Snyder.—First edition.
Pages   cm
Includes bibliographical references.
ISBN 978-1-61180-129-3 (alkaline paper)
1. Color in interior decoration—Handbooks,
manuals, etc. 2. Interior decoration—
Handbooks, manuals, etc. 3. House
furnishings—Handbooks, manuals, etc.
4. Handicraft—Handbooks, manuals, etc.
I. Title.
NK2115.5.C6N53 2014
747'.94—dc23
2013049310

FOR MY FRIEND SALLY LEE,
MUTUAL LOVER OF TEXTILES,
HOME, COLOR, AND CATS.

A good home must be made, not bought.

JOYCE MAYNARD

CONTENTS

INTRODUCTION

A HOUSE OF MANY COLORS

EVERY HOME HAS A STORY. EVERY FAMILY MAKES ITS OWN story in its home. I want to share with you the story of our colorful home and how it came to be.

Have you ever fallen in love at first sight? I did, the moment my husband, Mark, and I drove to the end of a dirt road in western Massachusetts to view the farmhouse where we now live. It was a clear, snowy February day, and I was pregnant with our daughter, Julia. We had been looking for a farm to move to so that we could raise our unborn child in the country, along with our flock of sheep and other animals. Once inside the old-fashioned Cape-style house, I could see the potential. The colors were all wrong for us, but I knew that the good bones of the sturdy house would make a great blank canvas for my art and my love of color.

Color runs through our lives here on our working sheep farm. Mark, Julia, and I tend over three hundred sheep and lambs. Most are a lovely creamy color, but some are shades of brown and gray. We raise them to help tame the land and fertilize the pastures, and we harvest their meat and wool. I keep a flock of exotic chickens for their eggs and for their colorful feathers that float around our landscape. We have three black-and-white Border Collies—Phoebe, Ness, and Kate—and a collection of colorful cats. To help us guard the sheep we keep a white Great Pyrenees guard dog named Winston, a gray guard donkey named Eeyore, and a dark brown guard llama named Jeremy.

The fields surrounding our farmhouse are full of colorful treasures to discover. In the spring, on a warm day, the old orchard all of a sudden explodes into the palest pink blossom. Bright yellow dandelions sparkle among the green grass, offset by purple violets. Salmon- and lilac-colored shrubs dot the landscape. In the summer, zinnias and cosmos bloom exuberantly. In the fall the sunflowers and autumn leaves blaze, singing the last hurrah of the New England growing season.

Our farmhouse is a magical, chaotic, colorful place full of love and animals, good food, warm, cozy fires, and creativity. Not everything is in its place, to say the least. Keeping clutter at bay is a full-time job. Piles of yarn and needles, graph paper, and swatches lie idle, waiting until I can find a spare moment to finish an

idea. Cans of paint and brushes wait for the next decorating or fabric project. On the kitchen stove, there is usually a pot of soup filling our home with an amazing aroma.

I believe a home's design should reflect the passions of the owner. Layers of years should build up as collections and experiences grow within a house. Too much pristine cleanliness makes for an uninteresting place—sterile and void and oh, so boring. A house should cause a visitor to ask questions. Everything should have a story—of a tale of discovery, of a trip gone wrong, of flat tires, of good food or bad, of eccentric shopkeepers and places to return to (or not). Decorating a house is an adventure and a creative exercise that takes thought, time, resources, and love. It doesn't happen overnight. Be patient and let your home grow. Build on the bones, and over the years it will morph and change and become better with time.

Our farmhouse will never really be "done." I go through fits and starts and spells of working on new ideas and decorations. Once in a while I'll be inspired to re-cover a piece of furniture in a new fabric. I like to think of my house as one giant art project that doesn't have a deadline. It's like a good stew simmering on the kitchen stove. I keep adding ingredients to make it better.

Color and textiles are my passions. My decorating budget isn't big, but what I lack in financial wherewithal I try to make up for with creativity. I am inspired by decorating magazines, historic houses, art museums, photos I have seen, places I have visited. I glean ideas and file away all that I see in my mental vault, never knowing when one of them will pop up to the fore to be incorporated, tweaked, and morphed into a decorating scheme in our home. I like to think outside the mainstream box of popular culture—not that I am avant-garde or anything like that. I like to be inspired by things in nature, places I have been, odd things from the past. I pile on layers of objects, colors, textiles, and experiences to create a feeling in our home of love and passion for things I find beautiful. A smooth river rock, a chair picked up from the side of the road, and scraps of antique fabric all have found a place in our home. I have learned that the making of a home cannot be hurried—it has to evolve, to grow with you, and to become you.

The thread of beautiful color combines with another passion, for the handmade—for things that are made by others' hands and things that I have made myself. I search out handmade objects at yard sales and flea markets. I may not ever know who made an object, in the past or in another land, but the mark of the maker's hand is visible within the piece. I cannot remember a time when I wasn't making something. When I was a child, my mother always requested that my sisters and I give her a gift that was made by hand. It didn't matter that it might not be perfect—it was from her kids' hands and the time spent making meant a great deal to her. The importance of making things has stuck with me all these years. It has become my reason to live—the creation and the sharing of handmade objects, including from-scratch cooking, hand-knit mittens, and a handcrafted home. Perhaps it will become yours, too.

Many homeowners hire professional decorators to take care of their interior decoration. There is nothing wrong with that, but I like to do it all myself. Nothing good in decorating happens instantly. Building a colorful home takes time and energy. Anyone with a charge card can purchase a room in a day from the Pottery Barn catalog. It takes an artist's eye, or a daring decorator-to-be, to take risks and step outside the everyday box of superstores, malls, and cookie-cutter catalogs. I think carefully about each room, how and when it will be used, and the mood I am trying to create. I search for ideas, clipping pages from magazines, picking through flea markets for a piece of inspiration. I visit decorative arts museums to educate my eye. I look at colors everywhere and wonder how they will translate into a space in our home. I think about our family and how we live. I dream about the colors and the fabrics and the paint treatment and the furniture I will keep looking for. I figure out how I can save money by making things myself that will look as though they came from a chic design store. I begin piling up notes (many only in my head) until they gel, and I can begin. I suppose I am really a decorator with one client—me.

I hope this book will show *you* how to put colors together fearlessly and help you decorate your home with beautiful, creative, and fun handmade projects. With

simple tools—paint, fabric, yarn, needles, and brushes—you'll be able to transform your home into a colorful masterpiece of your own. First, try making the projects just as I show you here. Just making your own handmade thing will give you confidence. The next time you will feel more courageous about tweaking the project with your own style. Take my ideas and put your own spin on them. As you learn each technique, you will find that each will inform the next. That is the fun of the handmade—to see where each project will take you, to wonder what is next, to discover what passion will become your next. I hope that you will find the same fascination, love, and fulfillment that I have by creating a handmade home of your own. It doesn't need to be perfect to begin with—the point is just to *begin*! Your home will grow and build upon itself and become your own colorful and creative place to share with your family and friends.

CH. 1

IN THE STUDIO

GETTING STARTED WITH COLOR AND MATERIALS

IF YOU ARE A CREATIVE PERSON, AND I KNOW YOU ARE because you are reading this book, you have probably always dreamed of having a studio of your own. "Studio"—that word to me means "creative space." Until I went to university, I did not know what a studio was. I had always sewn and crafted on a long table in my family's "back room" next to the washing machine and dryer. At school, I quickly discovered the allure and romance of the various studio spaces I was allowed to work in. Just walking into one made me feel creative—giving me the confidence that I could make something beautiful. A studio is a special space where paintings can be painted, quilts can be sewn, knits can be knit, music can be recorded. . . . A studio is a space for an artist of any kind to go to be creative, to get into the zone of making. It is a place to get messy and not feel guilty about the mess. After all, a studio is all about the mess.

I did not always have a studio. For most of my life I carved out a "faux studio" in another space in my home—a corner of a room with a table and a chair to sit at and a basket to keep my crafting, sewing, fiber, and art supplies collected together. It worked fine, but I always yearned for a real studio. Perhaps you want a studio space too?

Your studio can be any corner of your home that you can make into your creative space. If you do have an extra space in your home, I urge you to make it your own. It doesn't need to be big and fancy. It can be a closet, the attic, a garage, a corner of the basement or the kitchen. But mostly, build that studio in your head—carve out that space and make time to create. Work with your family or whomever you live with to let them know that creating is important to you. Let them know when you are in a creative mode, when you don't want to be bothered, and give them a time frame to leave you alone to create. What is necessary is to have a studio or creative space in your head—to have a spot where you file away ideas for future projects, things you want to learn and do and be.

Having a physical studio space is a real luxury and one I have worked toward for many years. My studio is on the ground floor of our farmhouse, set into the side of the hillside, below the porch. It has tall casement windows that take advantage of the natural southern exposure. Good light is very important for creating. If your space doesn't have nice windows, purchase really good "daylight" lamps to give you that daylight happy vibe. My studio's walls are covered with Homasote, a cellulose-based fiber wall board that functions as a giant bulletin board. These walls are covered with pictures and ideas that have been pinned up in a moment of "I must save this idea because it is beautiful" inspiration. The ideas become layered and tattered and covered by the next great idea. I painted the walls and trim white so they would be a blank canvas and not interfere with all the colors I work with when I am painting and designing textiles.

For the floor I used inexpensive, very durable, easy-to-clean vinyl composition tiles that are available in a dizzying array of colors. This is the floor covering that is used in many hospitals, grocery stores, and schools. I chose nine bright shades—chartreuse, pink, dark blue, sky blue, kelly green, orange, red, and purple—and laid them down with adhesive. The floor looks like a patchwork quilt. The doors are painted bright shades of turquoise and green, which coordinate with the floor tiles. The steps are painted fuchsia, and I have stamped a Moroccan-inspired design on them. The colorful floors and doors are the little sparks that give me a jolt of creativity when I walk in.

I have an assortment of cast-off chairs painted bright colors. My favorites are some discarded "teacher chairs" on wheels so that I can zip around between my computer and sewing machine. I made the table out of two "shop tables," with wheels on the legs, that I found at a junk store. They had been used at a silver factory that, sadly, went out of business after a couple of hundred years. I painted the tables periwinkle blue. Then I purchased a piece of smooth ¾-inch birch plywood, painted it white, and had it mounted on top of the two tables, to make one big table. The white tabletop makes a very useful surface for cutting fabric, painting, photography, and general crafts, and the bonus is that the table can be rolled around the room.

The space is very utilitarian, which I find inspirational. There are pots of paint, brushes, and knitting and crochet needles, pads of paper—all out and easy to find. There's a color printer, my computer, boxes of yarn, piles of fabric, and lists of ideas and things to make one day. There are piles of old art and discarded didn't-quite-work-out art, and there is usually a cat or two keeping me company. My family doesn't use the space—it's all mine to create what I want and to plan my next project. I know I am lucky, but so are you. Because you, too, can make your own studio space.

Now that you've got your creative studio percolating in your head and maybe in your home, it is time to start filling it with the tools and supplies you will be using to create a polychrome home. Let's look at some ideas that are important to consider and the physical supplies that I use and that you will need in order to begin.

LEARNING HOW TO USE COLOR
IN YOUR HOME

Let's start with color—glorious, radiant, bright, and happy color. The choice of the colors you use in your home is the most important decision you will make when decorating. Color is what you and your guests will see and feel as you walk through the door. Color is emotional—it can be fun, comforting, enveloping, jarring, safe, daring, or calm. The colors of your home, not how much something cost, are what your family and guests will remember most. I can still vividly recall the cantaloupe color that my mother painted on the walls in the living room of my first childhood home. The best thing about painted color is that it is easy to apply, and if you become unhappy with your choice, it can easily be painted over.

Many homeowners think only about resale. They choose their home's colors based on what realtors tell them will work for a quick sale. What a waste of time and beauty it would be for me and my family to live in a beige house. Where would the fun and excitement be without color? The warmth generated by a bright red, a blazing orange, a cool ocean blue, or a verdant spring green all add to the spiritual well-being of our family and those who visit. Our last home was painted pink with an electric blue door. Inside it was colored like a jewel box, and it sold in three days.

Get up your nerve and think outside the beige box. You will have to be comfortable with your choices and be able to live with them. Your family has to like them. Not every color you choose the first time will be exactly right, but the important thing is that *you have to start somewhere to learn where you are going.* Paint is cheap. If you don't begin, you'll never know what talents lie within you or what your home could have been. Be brave, be fierce. Learn to live and create with color with wild abandon.

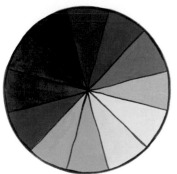

LEARNING ABOUT COLOR WITH THE COLOR WHEEL
An artist's color wheel is a great place to start learning about colors. I like to think of a color wheel as a rainbow in the round. Round and round the colors go, blending into the next one. A color wheel is a handy tool in your decorating arsenal.

ANALOGOUS COLOR COMBINATIONS
Analogous colors are those that are next to each other on the color wheel. Using such colors as yellow-green, yellow, yellow-orange, and orange in combination

will feel harmonious and safe and subtle. I used analogous colors in our living room. The yellow-gold walls, medium green chair rail, bright green bookcases, and chartreuse paneling opposite are all colors that are close together on the wheel. When we spend time in this room, it feels cozy, especially with the fire roaring in the middle of the winter.

COMPLEMENTARY COLOR COMBINATIONS

Complementary colors are those that are opposite each other on the color wheel. This is my favorite type of color combination. They just make my heart sing. Mother Nature sings the complementary love song like nothing else. Look around a garden and you'll see all kinds of fabulous complementary color combinations: pansies (yellow and purple), geraniums (red and green), petunias (red-violet and yellow-green), and sunflowers (orangey gold against a blue sky).

If you want to try out complementary color combinations but don't want to jump in as far as I have, consider adding pops of complementary colors. For example, imagine a royal blue velvet sofa against a robin's egg blue wall (analogous combination). By adding orange pillows (orange is complementary to royal blue) you get something fun and unexpected. Using a complementary color that isn't a true complement but a color that is just to the right or left of the true complement (such as the royal blue and orange) can create a great effect too.

TONAL COMBINATIONS

Shade or tone is the lightness or darkness of a particular color. The color red can range from the lightest pink (red with lots of white) to medium pink, to pure red and then darker to maroon (red with lots of black). Using shades of one color will create a subtle, softer feeling, such as in the pink bedroom in our home, where I use salmon-pink on the walls, pink on the woodwork, and pink Indian block-printed bedspreads.

USING NEUTRALS AND WHITES AS A BALANCE

Neutrals used in your home act as no color. White and black are two neutral shades. They are not represented on the color wheel. White is the absence of any color and black is all colors mixed together. Less extreme than white and black are other neutral colors. Beige, ecru, slate gray, taupe, umber, and sienna are made by mixing different amounts of colors from the wheel together, sometimes adding white to lighten. Perhaps that is why whites and beige are so popular—many

people can't decide what color to use so they just play it safe and opt for neutral. White comes in many tints—bluish whites, yellowy whites, pinky whites. Picking one to use can be just as hard as picking a real color.

When you look through the spaces in our home, they appear very colorful, but if you really observe, I have used many neutral shades to balance all the color. Many of the floors in our home are slate, natural pine, or painted neutrals. Choosing these colors, or leaving what was there in the form of natural wood, grounds a room in a sturdy neutral.

LOOKING AT COLOR

As a creative person interested in the decorative arts, you already know the colors you are attracted to. These are colors you have liked throughout your life, colors you gravitate toward, colors that make you feel happy and safe. Determining the colors that you want to use in your own home isn't quite as easy as picking a paint chip from a rack at the hardware store. It is important to realize how color works within your world and interior environment. Color is a function of light and how your eyes see it. Let's look at how it morphs and changes.

As the seasons change, the way different colors look to your eye will change. In winter, there is a coldness and rawness to the light. As spring approaches, the light begins to feel as though it is infused with energy. In summer, the light is strong but can be harsh. Autumn light is the prettiest—it is rich and full of warm gold undertones. The light also changes throughout the day. Your eye sees the same object differently in the morning, as the day progresses, and then toward evening. A fun experiment is to set out an object you love against a pretty background of green grass or stone. Observe the object several times during the day. You'll be amazed how it differs.

Colors also change to the eye when combined with a different color. Look at the photos here. Notice how the same sunflower gives you a different feeling when set on the different fabric backgrounds. Each of you will prefer a different color combination, but the important thing is to *see* the difference and determine what *you like*. The way a color appears to the human eye will change during the course of a year, even a day. The same goes for your home—the light pouring in your windows will change during the day and year. When choosing decorating colors, make sure that you are happy with your choices at the time of day and time of year you will be using the room most. I am drawn to the Oriental, Persian, and exotic colors of the Middle and Far East—darks and jewel tones. I have used these shades in our living room and library. The muted colors give a warm feeling. These are winter rooms, and the color definitely reinforces the cozy, warm factor.

On our porch I used lighter and brighter shades—they are more evocative of the summer season when we use the room. I love bright colors because they make me feel happy. I do realize that not everyone shares my exuberance for the bright and loud. If you are one of those people, take a second look at bright shades. They can be used in small bits to add punch and pizzazz to a space. Think of bright shades as the icing on the cake or the dangly earrings that enliven an outfit. They can add just the right bit of spark to energize a room. Once you begin using bright shades, you'll become more comfortable with them and be able to keep sprinkling them in your interiors to better effect.

TOOLS AND SUPPLIES FOR THE CREATIVE HOME

Over the years I have collected an arsenal of supplies that I use for decorating, crafting, and making things for our home, including paints, brushes, yarn, fabric, needles, and sewing and carpentry tools. Although this can be an expensive and mind-boggling process, if you collect your supplies slowly, you'll soon have all you need to keep decorating for years. It's important to store the items properly, keeping them away from water, pests, and extreme swings in temperature. Otherwise they may deteriorate and you may have to purchase them again.

PAINT

If you let me loose in a paint store without any fiscal restraint, I would purchase all kinds of paint and painting tools. I love going to a paint store, pawing through the pockets of color samples that can be made at the mixing station, and picking just the right shade for a project. Never one to throw anything away, I keep my partly used cans of paint in our basement, just in case I need to work on another project or touch up the old one. If you purchase one brand of paint in a certain finish, the colors can be mixed together to create your own special color recipe just when you need it. It is important to reseal all your paint cans; use a hammer or a mallet to tamp down the metal lids firmly. Otherwise they will dry out and become solid masses.

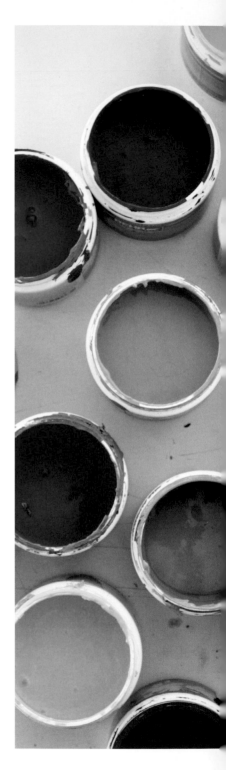

LATEX AND OIL-BASED HOUSE PAINTS

There are all kinds of paints available to the homeowner today, but prices and quality vary greatly. I like to purchase my paint from stores that have a very knowledgeable person who can steer me in the proper direction for my desired end use. Some paints are rather inexpensive, but my feeling is you get what you pay for. More expensive paints have more pigment and will cover in less layers, which saves me time. My favorite brand is Benjamin Moore; I have had lots of success with their paint over the years.

Most homeowners prefer latex paint for the ease of cleanup with water. There are many brands available, and I suggest trying several to decide upon your favorite. I prefer semi-gloss paint, as it is more durable than a matte finish and can be cleaned with soap and water. The rule of thumb is the shinier the paint, the more durable it is. Make sure you purchase paint for the situation you are using it in. Don't use an interior paint for an exterior job because it is not designed to withstand weather and water and it will fade. I use latex paint on my interior walls.

Oil-based paints are extremely durable. At one time, oil paints were the only kind of paint available. They go on very smoothly and brushstrokes disappear. Now, however, they are getting more and more difficult to purchase because of environmental laws. In many states they are only available by the gallon. If, like me, you prefer oil paints, you can purchase floor enamel, which is super durable but only available by the gallon. It can be tinted any color. Oil primer is still available in quart sizes and is a good choice for exterior uses. You can use oil-based primer under exterior latex paint but not vice versa.

Rust-Oleum is a brand of oil-based paint available in small cans that is useful for painting signs and metal and for exterior uses. It cannot be tinted the color of your dreams, although it is available in a large selection of colors. Marine paint, available where boatbuilders purchase supplies, is very durable and waterproof, but it is available in a limited number of colors. I prefer oil-based paints for furniture and high-traffic areas such as floors and doorways.

SPRAY PAINT

Spray paint is available in both water- and oil-based versions. The most common brands are Krylon and Rust-Oleum, and I have used both successfully. I have also used "farm enamel" paint, which comes in tractor colors such as John Deere Green and Allis Chalmers Red. It is extremely durable. Automotive supply stores sell many kinds of spray paint especially made for durability on metal. When using

spray paint, spray several light layers instead of fewer thick layers because the latter will drip. It dries quickly and is perfect for metal furniture, lamp bases, wicker furniture, and chairs.

CLEAR FINISHES

Homeowners use both water- and oil-based clear finishes to protect both painted and natural wood surfaces. Polyurethane is the most popular clear finish available for the homeowner, and it is water-based. It is available in matte and shiny finishes. Most people prefer it to oil-based finishes because of the ease and convenience of its water cleanup. I have had mixed results with polyurethane. In situations where there may be water damage, such as in the kitchen or on the floor, I suggest using an oil-based clear finish such as a varnish or an oil-based urethane instead, as it is much more durable.

Oil-based spar varnish is a favorite choice of boatbuilders. It protects well against damage caused by water and ultraviolet rays. I have used it on many of my projects including tabletops and the ceiling of our porch, and it holds up really well. It is surprisingly runny and so is applied in multiple thin coats. I apply three coats for good protection. It is also available as a spray. It is rather smelly, so apply it outdoors or when the windows can be open. Some people wear a respirator because of the fumes.

ARTISTS' ACRYLICS

I use artists' acrylics for painting the murals and faux wallpaper treatments in our home. Acrylic paint is made of acrylic polymer mixed with pigments. Artists' acrylics come in different grades: professional grade, which has more pigment in it; and student grade, which is cheaper to purchase and has less pigment. I use professional grade and have had good success with the Liquitex and Golden brands. The acrylic paint that is packaged in tubes (which is how I purchase them) is very thick—almost like peanut butter, but not as sticky. Acrylic paint can also be purchased in a fluid form in jars. Craft paints are acrylic paints that come in small tubes with a convenient squeeze spout and are available in a very large range of colors. They are not as thick as artists' acrylics. All of these paints can be mixed together and with latex paints. When painting wall murals, I intermix acrylics and latex paint. To thin them, I use water, taking care that they do not get so thin that they run when applied on a vertical surface. They can also be thinned with gel medium. They all clean up easily with water.

FABRIC PAINTS

There are many choices for fabric paint. I prefer the brands made by Jacquard Products and Pro Chemical and Dye Inc. They are available in transparent and opaque versions and also come in metallic colors. The painted fabric will have a reasonably soft hand and will become softer as it is washed. Follow the manufacturer's directions for dilution and heat-setting.

Fabric medium is an additive that can be added to any water-based paint, including latex house paint and acrylic paint. It makes the paint softer and thins it down for easier application to textiles. Fabric medium is an extremely inexpensive tool that turns ordinary latex paint into fabric paint. I have used it with great success, although the hand of the fabric so treated is still a bit stiff and the finish is opaque. Follow the manufacturer's directions for dilution and heat-setting.

PAINTBRUSHES AND PAINT APPLICATION TOOLS

There is a large selection of paintbrushes available at paint and home supply stores for applying paints and clear finishes, including natural and synthetic bristles and foam. Purchase the type of paintbrush recommended for the type of paint you are using—oil- or water-based. Refer to the packages or ask a paint specialist when choosing brushes.

It's nice to have a supply of one-, one-and-a-half-, and two-inch brushes on hand, including inexpensive bristle and foam styles. For oil paints, I prefer white china bristle brushes made by Purdy.

Artist brushes are very useful for many home painting projects and are available at craft stores. I prefer the Royal Soft Grip brand, which seems to work well for most of the uses I have. Purchase a selection of the following sizes and styles:

- Round brushes, sizes 2, 4, and 8
- Flat brushes, sizes 2, 4, and 8
- Liner brushes, sizes 0, 10/0, and 20/0

A stencil brush is also convenient for decorative techniques that involve stippling and pouncing, which is painting in short up and down strokes to create an uneven or spotted effect. You can make your own stencil brush by cutting the hairs short on a child's craft brush. You can use many household objects to execute textured decorative paint treatments, including plastic bags, rags, crumpled newspaper, bubble wrap, natural and synthetic sponges, and cotton swabs.

PAINTING TIPS AND TRICKS

Face it, painting can be a pain and a big mess. Over the years, I have learned many tricks that have made painting more fun and less hassle. They also make it possible to fit painting a coat or two in among the daily chores of life. Sometimes it is hard to set aside several hours to paint a room, but if you use some of these tips, you can fit a change of color into your regular daily life without upsetting your family's routines.

- Cleaning paintbrushes. If you need to take a break from painting and are too lazy to clean the brush or roller, wrap it in a plastic bag and store it in the freezer. Let it thaw before painting with it again.

- When rinsing a brush with water or paint thinner and changing colors, remove the excess paint and cleaner by tapping the brush quickly along the side of a bucket outdoors. You'll have a clean brush all ready to keep painting. Dry off excess moisture with a paper towel or rag so that you do not dilute the next color.

- Relegate a certain set of clothes to be painting clothes or wear a painting smock. This will save your wardrobe. If you do get either oil or latex paint on your good clothes, remove the spot immediately. Place a rag or paper towel under the stained fabric. Squeeze some dish detergent on the paint and brush it with a nail brush. It will disappear with a little scrubbing. You must remove it before the paint dries. When paint is dry, you can sometimes remove it with fine sandpaper if you are very careful not to rub too hard, which would make a hole in the fabric.

{Continued}

- Some colors are easier to cover than others. In general, yellow, orange, and red will take more coats to cover than other colors. When changing colors, painting any light color over a darker color will also take more coats. Remember this when planning a color change. An easy way to avoid having to do multiple coats of paint is to have a primer tinted your new color.

- If you choose to paint outside, check how buggy it is before beginning. Bugs of all kinds seem to be attracted to wet paint. It is a real bummer to check on your painted piece and find it decorated with flies and mosquitoes.

- To make identifying used paint cans easier, paint a stripe down the outside label before putting it away. Store cans so the stripe is easily seen. Be sure to keep the top clean, where the paint store affixes a label that shows the exact formula that was used to mix the paint.

TEXTILES AND SEWING SUPPLIES

Textiles are one of the most basic tools you will use to decorate your home. Textiles can be fancy and expensive, such as woven jacquard fabrics in beautiful patterns or shiny silks and velvets. Textiles can also be very basic workhorses such as kitchen towels, napkins, and tablecloths. There are many specialized supplies you'll need to collect to sew, work, and decorate with textiles. Scissors, needles, and sewing machines can be picked up at estate and yard sales. Make sure you keep scissors in a special place, away from your family; otherwise you may find your special sewing scissors used to clip the wet dog or, in my case, a dirty sheep.

FABRICS

Fabric has been one of my lifelong obsessions. I prefer using cotton, linen, wool, and natural fiber fabrics in my home decoration. I try to stay away from silk for use in my interiors, as it degrades in situations where there is a lot of natural light. I always prewash my cottons and linens before sewing because they usually shrink. For embroidery, I prefer stitching on 100 percent linen fabric. I also like to collect vintage fabrics, old clothing that can be cut apart, and remnants and damaged pieces. These fabrics and prints may be perfect for a small project I might like to make in the future.

THREADS AND NEEDLES

I use mercerized cotton embroidery floss, pearl cotton embroidery thread, and crewel and tapestry wool for hand-stitching. For beginners, I suggest wool, as it is very forgiving.

Chenille needles have a large eye and are easy to thread. Unlike tapestry needles they have a sharp point. They come in many sizes and are perfect for embroidery.

ADDITIONAL SEWING SUPPLIES

Any crafty home needs the following supplies:

- **A BASIC SEWING MACHINE.** My Bernina 831 is almost forty years old. It does straight stitch and zigzag and that's about it. Look for used machines on eBay or at yard sales. Although there are many new, expensive, computerized sewing machines available that are capable of doing hundreds of stitches and embroidery, you need not spend thousands of dollars when just beginning. New machines are made with plastic parts. I prefer older machines that weigh more because they are made with metal parts that are more durable. You may find you can even get by on an antique treadle straight stitch sewing machine. Most sewing machines can be fixed as long as parts are still available.
- **SEWING AND CRAFT SCISSORS.** Keep a pair of scissors exclusively for fabric and a less expensive pair for cutting paper and for general crafts. Kids' scissors are inexpensive, and I keep a pair in each room that I work in.
- **GRAPH RULER.** A clear ruler available at art supply and quilting stores in different sizes is extremely useful.
- **AN AUTO-FADE OR VANISHING MARKER FOR FABRICS.** Available at quilting stores. I use these markers to draw embroidery designs. They will fade over time or with a spritz of water.
- **STEAM IRON AND IRONING BOARD.**
- **KNITTING NEEDLES, CROCHET HOOKS, AND EMBROIDERY HOOPS IN VARIOUS SIZES.**

YARN

For knitting and crocheting, I prefer 100 percent wool and blends of sheep's wool and other animal fibers. I have my own line of yarn, called Color By Kristin, which is available in a stunning color palette. It is made of a luxurious blend of 50 percent wool, 25 percent alpaca, and 25 percent mohair.

PUTTING IT ALL TOGETHER:
COLLECTING INSPIRATION

Now that you know what supplies you will need to collect, let's look at how to find color and style ideas for your home. Most likely you have many of these ideas deep within you. It is a matter of opening up your idea well and getting the ideas out into the open in physical terms. None of this is hard to do—it is just a matter of giving yourself some time to think and to conceptualize the colors and style of your home.

Start by answering the following questions:

1. What are your favorite colors? What colors have you been lusting over for the past year? Have you seen colors in decorating magazines and online that appealed to you?
2. What individual colors give you an emotional response? Blue may make you feel safe and secure. Yellow may make you feel happy and optimistic.
3. What kind of emotion are you going for in the room you are planning? Write down your thoughts about different colors and develop the ideas over time.

The easiest way to tailor the color theme for a room is by a starting with a fabric choice. Begin with a single fabric or a collection of fabrics you love and build the paint colors and other fabric textures around it. Layer similar color fabrics in graphic stripes, plaids, chevrons, polka dots, florals, and other organic motifs to create a warm and inviting atmosphere.

If you are at a loss as to where or how to begin, tear pages out of magazines or develop pin boards using sites such as Pinterest or software such as Evernote. Remember that computer monitors, tablets, and phones have backlit screens, so colors look different on them than in reality. A physical object—a picture from a magazine, a catalog, a postcard from a museum shop, a piece of art, or a fabric—gives you something concrete to work from. Collect these objects and keep them in a file, or a shoebox, until you are ready to begin. You will quickly see a theme developing and you will be able to build a room or a home through the photos you have collected.

Making up a board of ideas—grouping certain colors and textures together—is something many professional designers do to develop their room concepts. A

board such as this is called a "mood board," and it is very helpful as you are planning the colors and decoration in a room. Besides, it is fun to make. Begin with an inexpensive corkboard. Pin your inspirations from your files to the board. Add fabrics, ribbons, threads, and yarns you have found. Ask your family for comments as your ideas and the mood board progress. Keep adding layers—there are never too many ideas.

Once your ideas begin to solidify, you will start to feel more confident about the color direction your project is going to take. It's time to head to the paint and fabric store. Take your mood board with you and collect paint chips that you can take home and play with and add to your mood board. Using the paint chips, combine different colors and tape them to a piece of white cardboard. Set them in the room where you plan to use the colors. Observe how the colors look at different times of the day. You'll notice that during daylight hours, the colors will give you one emotional response and later, when the room is lit with artificial lights, you'll get a different vibe. If you are coloring a room that will be used for dinner with candlelight, you should observe the samples with lit candles too.

Paint companies make it so easy now to experiment with colors. They also produce small jars of paint samples. Purchase some of the sample jars and paint a piece of hardboard with a small foam roller. The hardboard has a similar finish to a wall. Most home centers will cut hardboard for you into smaller pieces. You'll want to do the number of coats of paint on the hardboard that you plan for the walls. The painted piece of hardboard can be moved from room to room so you can observe the color in different areas of your home. Many times, I have picked a color I thought would work in one room, only to be unhappy with the actual effect. Later, I have been able to use it in a different room. Having a painted movable hardboard gives you flexibility. The hardboard panel can be painted over many times as you are working on your color stories for each room in your home.

If you are planning a large project that will be covered with fabric, such as a couch or chair, purchase a sample yard first. (Although fabric stores will supply you with small swatches, they are not large enough to get the real feeling of a piece of fabric.) Leave the fabric in the exact spot that the furniture will live in and observe it over a couple of weeks, how you react to it in different light conditions, and so forth. Fabric and the labor involved to upholster a piece are much more expensive than paint, so make sure you will be happy with your choice.

HOW TO SELECT A
COLOR PALETTE FOR YOUR HOME

BECAUSE COLOR WILL BE THE SINGLE MOST IMPORTANT choice you make in each room in your home, it is important to start experimenting with it so that you feel more confident with choosing and combining colors. At first you might feel awkward, but the more you work with colors, the easier it will become. Just like riding a bike, the hardest time is in the beginning. After a while, it will become old hat.

A color palette is a group of colors that are combined together to create a pleasing collection. The word comes from the fine-art world where painters use a stiff board, called a "palette," to arrange and mix paint. When selecting the color palette for your home, it is best to begin with one room and then work your way through your home, room by room. Begin with the room you feel most comfortable with—perhaps a small room such as a bathroom or a bedroom. Think about what feeling you want the room to convey and then choose a base color. Then choose a few more colors that you think will complement the base color. If you are stuck and not sure how to choose a color, begin with a multicolor fabric choice that might make a nice curtain, pillow, or bedcover. Using the fabric, match up the different colors in the fabric with the same shades from the paint chips. Chances are the colors from your favorite fabric are also going to look good together as paint choices. Pull out one shade to use as your base wall color and then use the other shades as accent colors. Consider also the possibility of veering away from the fabric colors by choosing lighter and darker colors in the same tones as on the fabric.

Once you feel comfortable pulling colors from a fabric, try this color exercise.

It is a fun and easy way to play with color using free materials. Once you work with the paint chips, try doing the same exercise with yarn, fabric, oil paints, and watercolors. The more you play with color, the more confident you will become.

SUPPLIES

- Paint chips from paint stores
- Scissors
- Cardstock
- Double-sided tape

1. Cut the individual paint chips apart, removing any white space between the squares of color. Lay the squares out on a table.

2. Begin arranging them in a grid, moving them around, playing with the colors to see which look nice together. Once you get an arrangement that is to your liking, use the double-sided tape to attach them to the paper. Hang it on your wall or mood board as decoration and inspiration.

LAYERING COLORS TO CREATE DECORATIVE PAINT TECHNIQUES

SUPPLIES

- White latex primer
- Cardstock, cardboard, or hardboard
- A selection of small test jars of latex paint, as follows: 1 base color in a light shade, 3 analogous colors in shades slightly darker than the base color, 1 top color in a shade related to the other colors (see Note)
- 1-inch foam paintbrush
- 4 deli containers
- Texturizing materials such as rags, sponges, or plastic bags
- Water for cleanup

ONCE YOU'VE SELECTED YOUR BASIC PALETTE, YOU CAN GIVE your walls or furniture more depth and interest by layering colors on top of each other. Many of the walls in our home were painted with different paint-layering techniques. Let's see how to choose the colors to layer by experimenting with a group of colors. The last time you did an experiment like this may have been in elementary school art class. Think of how much fun it was then. Now you can use the color wheel on page 5 as your guide for combining colors. If you layer yellow on orange, you will get orange-yellow. If you layer two colors that are opposite each other on the wheel—complementary colors—you will get brown!

You can use your walls as a giant mixing palette. By layering colors on a wall, as an artist working in oils does on her canvas, you can create nuanced, beautiful, dreamy shades. If you were to paint a room yellow, then layer bits of related analogous colors on the wall, and finish with a light orange wash, you would end up with a subtle-looking gold color. That is what I did on the walls in my living room to produce a Tuscan gold (see page 105). My goal was to make the wall look random and textured. Treating walls like this gives an interesting, imperfect look—prettier than a flat, one-color treatment—and is really fun to do. Paint treatments like this also hide dings and scratches, making them perfect for high-traffic areas (see the stairway in "How to Colorwash a Wall," page 177).

NOTE: Whatever color you choose as the topcoat will be the dominant color on the wall. The colors below will add to the color feeling but will be covered by the topcoat.

1. Use the primer to prime your cardboard surface. This will ensure that the colors you paint on the board will be true and also will not soak into the surface.
2. Cover the primed surface with your base color. Let it dry.

3. Pour a small amount of each analogous color into a deli container and thin down with water to the consistency of cream.

4. Dip a rag, sponge, or a crumpled plastic bag into one of the colors. Lightly pounce, drag, or streak the thinned color onto your painted board. Do not cover the surface entirely; just add random textured bits of color.

5. Repeat with the other 2 analogous shades. There is no need to let the paint dry between adding these colors. Let the board dry.

6. Thin the paint for the topcoat in a deli container. Using a rag, soak up the thinned paint. Rub the paint over the surface as if you were washing a floor, to create a color wash. Let it dry. If you are happy with the outcome, let it be. If you want it darker and more opaque, add another washed layer. If you want it lighter, add a small bit of white paint to the top color and wash the surface again.

7. This is not an exact science. It is best to keep notes as you go so that you can repeat the same process on your walls.

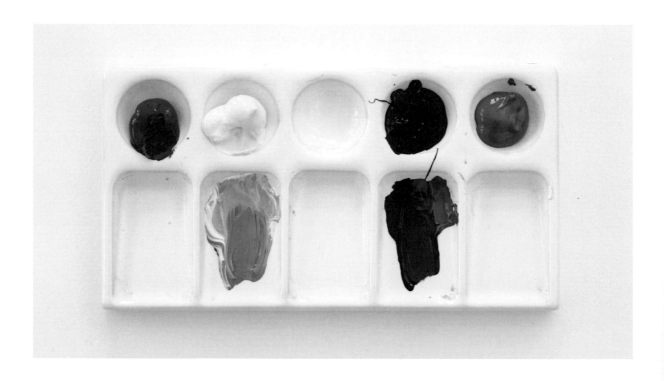

WHERE I FIND
DECORATING IDEAS

My favorite places to find decorating ideas are in shelter magazines such as *The World of Interiors, British Country Living, Elle Décor,* and *House Beautiful.* Through these magazines, I learn of new interior decorating books, which I can frequently borrow from the library. I like to look at interiors as shown on some websites, but I find that I don't absorb ideas from a computer screen as readily as from the printed page. For those who live in urban areas, decorator's show houses are a fun way to see current trends.

My favorite idea source is visits to house museums to see how others lived. I find the homes of artists interesting because they always seem to have handmade touches that are individual to their own houses. Here's a list of favorite house museums near my home that I have found inspiring. Check in your local area for historic homes as sources of inspiration.

OLANA, the home of Frederic Edwin Church, Hudson, New York

ORCHARD HOUSE, the home of Louisa May Alcott, Concord, Massachusetts

FRELINGHUYSEN MORRIS HOUSE AND STUDIO, Lenox, Massachusetts

CHESTERWOOD, home and studio of the sculptor Daniel Chester French, Stockbridge, Massachusetts

AUGUSTUS SAINT-GAUDENS'S HOME AND STUDIO, Cornish, New Hampshire

MARK TWAIN HOUSE AND MUSEUM, Hartford, Connecticut

CH. 2

THE GARDEN

AND

ENTRYWAYS

OUR FARMHOUSE WAS BUILT IN 1751, BACK IN THE EARLY
days of the settling of North America. It sits at the end of a dirt road in the rolling
hills of western Massachusetts. From the outside, our house looks like any normal
New England Cape-style farmhouse (a Cape is a one-and-a-half-story house
with no attic). Like many farmhouses, ours has been added on to over the years.
I love the sense of history that our house has. The antique structure is made of
giant beams of wood, hand hewn with axes. The foundation is fieldstone that was
moved in place with oxen. An ell was added to the original Cape in the 1940s. In
the 1970s, a rustic porch was added, which had a cement pad. In 2010, we tore the

porch down and added a two-story, three-season porch and a basement studio on the existing cement pad. Our house is the product of many families' changes over 250 years. I often wonder at all that occurred in this house before we moved in—but only the house knows.

The approach to the farmhouse is from the north, and it is tucked neatly into the landscape. It is painted white and has a gray cedar-shake roof bordered with a copper snow belt to shed the snow (a shake is a shingle made by splitting, not sawing, wood). New England is the land of white farmhouses. I feel it is important for a house to fit architecturally and visually into the character of its neighborhood and region, so we chose to paint our home white so that it would assimilate into the rural character of our area. The only signs of the artist owner and of the color within are the brightly colored doors. Each entryway is a different color—red, teal blue, kelly green, orange, and citrus yellow. I like to change the colors every few years. Changing the color of a door is easy to do and can completely transform the look and feel of an entryway.

Our farmhouse faces south—the traditional New England way to position a building to take advantage of the sun's path. I had never paid much attention to the direction of the sun in my other homes, which were in suburban areas. Living here in the countryside with an open expanse of land has made me more attentive to the way the light changes during the day and the year. On the south side of our farmhouse, there is a large open lawn leading to the sheep pastures and an apple orchard that was abandoned over twenty-five years ago. It is a perfect spot for my flower and vegetable garden. As the years have gone by, my gardening interests have moved more toward planting ornamental flowers and herbs, with just a few vegetables for our use. It makes me happy to have zinnias, sunflowers, amaranth, and more for abundant summer and fall bouquets.

As we were settling into our home about fifteen years ago, I began creating seating areas outside to function as places to sit, read, and entertain. The term "outdoor rooms" has become a trend in the shelter world. Depending on where and how you live, they can be a real source of pleasure. One of my favorite places to sit is just beside my flower garden under a rustic pergola that is covered with grapevines. The vines supply shade from the sun, and the rusty metal furniture I picked up at a local auction is perfect to sit on while I prepare flowers for indoor vases.

Outbuildings add a sense of history to a house. Farmhouses like ours had large barns for the animals. Unfortunately, the old barn on this farm burned to the ground in the 1960s. When you are a gardener and a farmer, you have a lot of tools. I designed a simple garden shed complete with a narrow porch to house my garden stuff. I wanted the outbuilding to feel like a little house. I used salvaged windows to give it a cottage feeling. I stained it a mossy green color to fit into the landscape and painted the door a contrasting shade of orange. You can buy many similar garden sheds and have them trucked in. I like to support my local builders, so I had the shed built from scratch.

Outdoor rooms do not have to be costly. For one of my seating areas closer to my studio, I made a table out of an old iron sewing machine base. I attached a piece of ½-inch plywood and topped it with a large slab of white Vermont marble I had picked up years before. Arranged around the marble table are four metal chairs that I bought at a secondhand store.

Since the late 1980s I have kept a flock of laying hens to provide fresh eggs and roosters and guinea hens for their pleasant-sounding crows and chatter. Chickens don't need glamorous quarters—just a basic shed to protect them from the weather and to keep them safe from predators. The "chicken palace" is built out of scraps of plywood, siding, windows, and doors that I saved from various building projects. I painted the coop traditional barn red to continue the old-fashioned exterior color scheme. The signs were painted on scraps of wood. Chickens are an efficient way to recycle garden and kitchen waste and create fertilizer that is completely local to a farm.

When you drive up to our house you see a small barn that is painted traditional barn red. In it we keep freezers full of lamb, which we sell at our local farmers' markets through our locally grown meat business, Leyden Glen Lamb. In a small bay, there is a self-serve farm stand where customers can purchase our farm-raised lamb (we also sell our lamb at nearby farmers' markets in Northampton and Amherst). These kinds of businesses are common in the countryside and make an excursion to the farm an adventurous outing for our customers. When I designed our lamb logo, I wanted to use complementary colors and link them to the green pastures that our sheep graze. I chose pea green and bright pink, and the label stands out against the color of the meat. I carried the pea green logo color through on exterior signs I hand-painted and hung on the barn and chicken shed. It is fun to add an "identity" to any home. For us, it is our sheep farm, but for you it may be your dogs or cats or your garden. Painting handmade signs gives a special individual touch to a home or outbuilding.

Using landscape and hardscape materials that are found locally makes sense financially and aesthetically. Goshen stone is a blue-gray schist stone that was used years ago to make a walkway that leads to the front door of our farmhouse. I wanted more of the same stone around the house, and luckily the quarry was still in business. I ordered a few dump-truck loads of stone to build a patio close to the cellar door, just outside my studio. Although the patio has been in place for a little over a decade, it looks as though it was built at least fifty years ago. Metal chairs are best for outdoor seating areas. They don't rot like wood, and they don't have to be put away in the winter. It will take a very long time for them to rust. Colorful cushions can be made to soften the seats. The stone patio is furnished with a big round table. Around the table, I have black metal Parisian-style "boing boing" chairs. Pots of colorful annuals are scattered around the patio. In the summer, it is a nice place to have drinks by candlelight.

HOW TO PAINT
AN EXTERIOR DOOR

IT IS FUN TO PAINT EXTERIOR DOORS IN SEVERAL DIFFERENT colors. I use exterior-grade latex or oil-based paint. Exterior paint is formulated to weather better and protect the wood from water; it is also more resistant to ultraviolet light exposure and damage. This is a project that can be tackled in a weekend and it gives an instant hit of change and drama to any home's entryway. Choose a sunny day when you can leave the door open to dry overnight, or begin early in the morning. Latex paint will dry rather quickly, but it is smart to leave the door open so it can cure. Oil paint needs several hours to dry. Some people remove their doors and hardware to paint them, placing them horizontal on sawhorses. I just work around the hardware and double-check for dripping paint.

NOTE: I prefer Zinsser Bullseye 1-2-3 Primer for both exterior and interior paint jobs. I prefer glossy paint for doors because it washes easily.

1. Put a dropcloth on the ground under your door.
2. Using a putty knife and sandpaper, loosen and remove any flaking paint. Wearing gloves and goggles, use TSP and hot water to wash the door and remove mildew and dirt. Let dry thoroughly.
3. Using primer, paint any raw spots of wood. Let dry.
4. Using exterior paint, paint the door. Begin at the top of the door and follow the grain of the wood, painting each panel separately. (See illustration.) Carefully paint around the hardware with the small artist's brush. Remove any drips. Paint the narrow sides of the door. You can paint the door surrounds to match the door or leave them as they were originally. It is up to you.
5. Let dry and repeat. Sand lightly before applying the next coat of paint, and wipe with a tack cloth to remove all sanding residue. Some colors will not cover in two coats, and it may be necessary to paint the door several times.

SUPPLIES

- Dropcloth
- Putty knife
- 150 grit sandpaper and tack cloth
- 2-inch paintbrush
- Small artist's brush
- Exterior primer (see note)
- Exterior paint (see note)
- TSP (trisodium phosphate) and rags, for washing door
- Rubber gloves and safety goggles

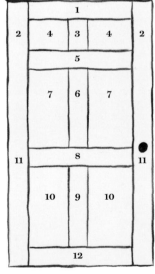

Step 4

COLORFUL OUTDOOR SIGNS

SUPPLIES

- Piece of recycled wood or metal such as a cabinet door
- Screwdriver if needed to remove old hardware
- Putty knife
- Foam sanding block
- 100 grit sandpaper
- Electric orbital sander
- Wood filler
- Primer (exterior primer if the sign will be outdoors)
- Paint in an assortment of colors (fade- and water-resistant exterior paint for an outdoor sign)
- 1-inch paintbrush and artist brushes
- Power drill and wood screws or eye hooks and 18-gauge wire, for mounting

OUR FARMHOUSE LOOKS VERY TRADITIONAL FROM THE OUT-side, except for the colored doors. Besides the doors, the only other clue that an artist may live within is the different exterior signs I have painted and hung. Signs are easy to make, using recycled cabinet doors, furniture, and scraps of wood. Scrap pieces of metal are great, too, because they will not rot like wood. Think up some fun phrases that you might like to paint to add a bit of whimsy and color to your own home.

1. If you are using an old piece of wood or a recycled door, remove all old hardware. Use a putty knife to loosen any flaking paint. Use an electric sander, followed by hand-sanding with the foam block, to smooth out any odds and ends of paint. Use wood filler and a putty knife to fill any holes in the wood. Let the filler dry and sand it lightly with sandpaper.

2. Prime your sign with a basic primer. Prime both the front and back of your sign so that it will be completely protected from moisture.

3. Using your chosen color of paint, cover your sign with two layers, letting it dry completely between coats.

4. Using an artist's brush and your own handwriting, paint the words you'd like to convey to guests and strangers.

5. To hang your sign, drill pilot holes into the sign and use wood screws to mount. Alternatively, drill pilot holes, screw in eye hooks, and run a piece of thick wire through the hooks to hang.

MOSAIC FLOWERPOTS

I HAVE A WEAKNESS FOR DISHES, AND ON EACH TRIP I TAKE, I usually find a potter who makes colorful pots and bring some home. I also collect old dishes in pretty colors and patterns from flea markets and yard sales. When they break, I cannot bear to throw them out. I began saving them at least a decade ago, stashing them in the basement in the hopes of using them for mosaic work. I have been intrigued by the pique assiette *technique, which uses shards of broken dishes to make new things—whether they're new vases or pots, walls, or buildings. To find out more about the art of mosaics, do some Web searches using these key words: Maison Picassiette, Antoni Gaudí mosaic, Grandma Prisbrey's Bottle Village, the Little Chapel, Guernsey. You, too, will be inspired to save your broken dishes!*

Making a mosaic-covered flowerpot is a messy project best done outside or in a space that can get wet and dirty. Give yourself several days to complete this project. First you will break your dishes into small pieces called shards. With a gluelike substance called mastic, you will attach them to the pot. Finally, you will fill the empty spaces with grout, which will hold them onto the pot.

1. Cover your work surface with towels or a dropcloth. Wearing safety goggles and gloves, wrap your broken pottery in a towel and hit it with a hammer hard enough to break it up but not so hard as to smash it into smithereens. Use the tile nippers to shape the broken ceramic and china shards into smaller pieces. Place the nipper blades no more than ¼ inch from the edge of the shard and squeeze to break the shard into smaller pieces. The shards should be between ½ and 1½ inches in diameter. If they are any larger, it is difficult to cover the convex surface of the pot. Sort your shards by color.

2. Clean and dry your pot before working with it. If it's an older pot that has had dirt and plants in it, use bleach to clean it.

3. Wearing rubber gloves, apply a layer of mastic about ¼ inch thick to the terra

SUPPLIES

- Dropcloth
- An old towel
- Safety goggles
- Tile nippers
- Broken ceramic plates and bowls and other old china
- Terra cotta flowerpot (new pots work best)
- Hammer
- Mastic (acrylic tile adhesive, available at your local hardware or home improvement store)
- Putty knife or artist's palette knife
- Premixed tile grout
- Rubber or latex gloves
- Bucket and water
- Large sponge (not cellulose)
- Scotch-Brite heavy-duty scouring pad

cotta pot with an artist's palette knife or a putty knife. Work a 5-inch-square section at a time. Coat the back of your pottery shard with mastic and firmly push it onto the mastic on the pot. When working with rounded shards from bowls or pitchers, decide on which side you want to feature. Typically bowls are highly decorated on the inside or convex shape of the piece and pitchers are decorated on the outside or concave shape. Either shape can be applied to the pot, but when applying concave shapes, fill the entire opening with mastic to attach it. The spacing between the different-sized and -shaped shards will vary, but aim for ¼- to ⅓-inch spacing. Wipe away any excess mastic that has oozed out from under the shards.

4. Continue until your entire pot is covered with shards. You can make patterns with the pieces by arranging them by color or in stripes. I work half the pot one day and the other half the next day. Let it dry overnight or for several days.

5. The pot can be grouted as soon as the mastic is dry, or later. It doesn't matter. Wearing gloves, scoop up a small amount of grout with your fingers and slather it into the spaces between the shards. Build up the grout over the sharp edges of the concave pieces of tile. Try not to get too much grout on the pottery shards so that cleaning the finished surface will be easier. Work a small section at a time. Using a wet sponge, smooth out the grout, taking care not to remove too much of it. Let it dry overnight. When working a larger pot, I grout a small section each day.

6. When the grout is dry, clean off any grout residue on the surface of the shards with a Scotch-Brite scouring pad.

7. Let the pot dry completely for at least a week before filling with potting soil and plants. In the winter, remove the soil and store the pot indoors or under cover.

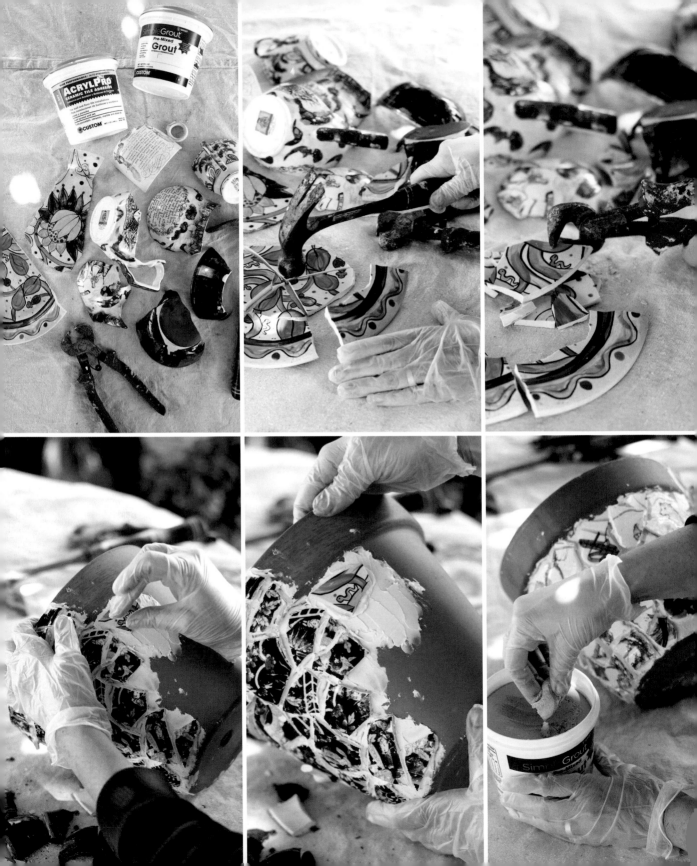

Mosaic
Flowerpots

PAINTED TERRA COTTA POTS

SUPPLIES

- Terra cotta flowerpots (new pots work best)

- Oil-based primer

- China bristle brush, for priming with oil-based primer

- Paint thinner, for cleaning brush

- 1-inch foam brush, for painting main colors

- Latex paint in pink, turquoise, ultramarine blue, medium blue, bright yellow, fuchsia, lime green, and dark brown

- Artist brushes in assorted sizes for painting designs

- Artist's liner brush, size 10/0

- Spar varnish

ALTHOUGH I HAVE LOTS OF SPACE TO PLANT FLOWERS ON our property, I always like to have some colorful flowers in pots that can be moved around to add color where and when I want it. To add more color and a fun and bright look to your yard, paint terra cotta pots in bright colors. This is a project that can be as detailed as you want. Kids can help, too.

1. Clean and dry your pot before painting. If it's an older pot that has had dirt and plants in it, use bleach to clean it.

2. Paint the inside and outside of the pot with the oil-based primer. Let it dry overnight.

3. Using the latex paint, paint the outside of each pot in your chosen base color. Let dry. When dry, paint the rim of the pot in another shade. Paint a second coat on both rim and base.

4. Decide on your motifs. I used simple motifs including polka dots, stripes, chevrons, and undulating lines. (Refer to the photo for the placement of the motifs I used.) Using freehand brushstrokes, paint the designs in your chosen colors on the outside of the pot. Let dry. If the design color does not cover the base color, repeat with another layer of paint.

5. When dry, use a liner brush and a dark color (I used dark brown) to paint the outline of each motif.

6. If your pot is going to be used in a garden outside and will be exposed to weather, paint or spray it with spar varnish. Apply at least three coats, letting the sealant dry overnight between coats.

7. If you aren't opposed to natural aging, you can let your pot fade. The paint may eventually flake off. If you live in a cold climate, store your pot indoors during the winter. Better yet, bring your pots inside and keep houseplants in them.

SUNFLOWER INSPIRATION

Mark and I have been growing sunflowers for almost a decade. It began when we bought a piece of farmland to grow hay on. I went along with the purchase with the caveat that we would grow some sunflowers along the road as a visual gift to our neighbors. Over the years, the sunflower field grew in size, and I became more and more interested in the different varieties of sunflowers that are available as seeds for home gardeners to plant.

Throughout art history, sunflowers have been favorite flowers featured in wood engravings, paint, folk art, wallpaper, and fabric design. The most iconic sunflower image of recent art history is of course Van Gogh's sunflower series. It is no wonder Van Gogh painted such beautiful flowers in the paintings he made in Arles in 1888 in southern France. The outward simplicity of yellow petals and a large center draw any flower lover or artist in. When you actually look closely at a sunflower bloom, you realize that the center is actually made up of thousands of little flowers, each of which grows into a seed that can be eaten by birds and humans or pressed to release oil used for cooking. As the flower grows and ages, its short life cycle takes on almost human traits—from sprouted seedling to proud and perky, almost blooming stalk to gorgeous bloom, then to mature seed head and finally to bent-over age, when it decomposes into the soil from where it sprouted. Sunflowers are truly amazing and beautiful flowers.

Sunflowers are very easy to grow if you have adequate sun. Depending on the variety, they bloom in as few as fifty days from germination or as many as 110 days. There are single-stem and branching varieties. Single-stem sunflowers have one large flower per plant. Multibranching sunflowers can produce as many as fifty blooms over the growing season. Flower breeders have engineered short sunflowers (less than 2 feet tall) and very tall sunflowers (more than 14 feet). Plant sunflowers when all chance of frost is past. Because of the differing germination time and "dates to bloom," it is possible to have sunflowers in bloom from June all the way until the first frost.

CH. 3

THE

KITCHEN

A KITCHEN IS THE HEART OF MOST FAMILY HOMES — FULL
of good smells, family news, and constant activity. Our kitchen is the nerve center of
family life, the place where Julia's homework gets done, mail lands, meals get cooked
and consumed, stories shared, bills paid, flowers arranged, and where little lambs
are taken to warm up and be revived during lambing season. I want my guests to feel
that they are very welcome and that they never want to leave our kitchen.

When we purchased our home, the kitchen was in the basement. It was an odd
setup, but it must have worked well for the family who located it there. We knew
it didn't feel right for us and so I set about moving the kitchen to the main floor of
the farmhouse. We decided to knock out the walls separating three small bedrooms
to make one room, a kitchen, on the main floor of our house. I began designing the
kitchen as I begin most projects—with a tape measure, some graph paper, and a
pencil and eraser. I thought carefully about the needs of each family member and,
most important, how I cook in the kitchen and what my needs are as head chef and
bottle washer. I began with a wish list, which I suggest everyone do when renovat-
ing a kitchen. At the top of my list was a window over the sink so I could look out,
as I work, at the seasons changing, at sheep grazing and chickens pecking.

THE WAY TO COOK

It is really nice to incorporate old family pieces, if you are lucky enough to have them, into new spaces. I designed the kitchen around my mother-in-law's large antique corner cupboard. It was passed down to us when she died and has always held a special place in our home. It is large and sturdy and holds all our everyday dishes. I measured the cabinet, and drew and planned the rest of the kitchen around this two-hundred-year-old piece, which most likely was built by a farmer for his house. The other piece of furniture I designed the kitchen around was my German immigrant grandmother Frieda's 1920s Sellers cabinet (a portable kitchen cabinet similar to the Hoosier). My grandmother was a fabulous baker, cook, and needlewoman, and I was determined to bring her spirit and cupboard into our kitchen. These cabinets were popular before built-in cabinetry became more common and edged them out.

I began falling for unfitted kitchens (without built-in cabinets) when I saw them in England and on the pages of British *Country Living*. I wanted to combine hardworking, new cabinets that looked old-fashioned with our special heirloom pieces. I found a cabinetmaker who would take my graph paper drawings and copy the British style of deep drawers and large wooden knobs. They used old-fashioned milk paint for the finish. I used a wide, deep, white fireclay farmhouse sink from England and topped it with old-fashioned-looking but new taps and faucet. I went to a local company, Ashfield Stone, to pick out a piece of blue-gray schist from their quarry to top one of the new cabinets. Schist is a type of stone that comes in many colors. In New England, it is a dark bluish-gray and has stripes and splotches of brown, silver, and white throughout. For the island, a friend made a thick, sturdy top of maple. I enjoy telling visitors the story of how the different bits and pieces of our kitchen came about. It's a process that is fun to plan and then bring to fruition.

I am a bit obsessed with light fixtures. When I look in interior decorating magazines, I always notice light fixtures with character. Interesting lights really make a room, and it is worth the extra work to find lighting fixtures that can't be found in a mass-market home store. I began haunting antiques stores and flea markets. A good electrician can retrofit any old fixture or object to make a working light. The wrought-iron light over the kitchen table is an old oil lamp. I brought the iron light with an opalescent glass shade, which is now over the island, home from a trip to the UK. I have seen all kinds of things used for lighting. Put on your thinking cap: pails, colanders, baskets, machine parts—all can be transformed into creative light fixtures.

We have two seating areas in our kitchen. The first is around a worn old oak table that came from my hometown. The veneer is shot, but I can't part with the table because it has been our table since we were first married. A friend once told me to get newer kitchen chairs because they will be sturdier than antiques. I found our set of Hitchcock-style chairs at a secondhand store. A Hitchcock-style chair is a traditional New England chair that is painted black and decorated with gold-colored flowers and leaves. Often there are fancy turnings that are also banded in gold. Some have cane or rush seats, and some are plain wood. The hand-woven rush seats on the chairs I picked up are getting rather frayed by the cats, so I have sewn chair pillows for them from digitally printed fabric of my own design.

Long ago, I saw in a magazine a photo of a kitchen with a wing chair in it. The chair made the space look so inviting and comfy. I copied that photo memory and used a wing chair from Mark's grandmother Nina to add that bit of comfort to our kitchen table. It's a favorite spot for everyone to sit. It needs to be re-covered because the cats use it for a scratching post. I wrap the cushion in different Indian block-print fabrics to add to the mishmash of patterns. In the far corner of the

I like a good bit of worn patina in a home. "Patina" is the decorating term for an aged look. It can be developed over time or hurried by paint techniques such as dragging and distressing a finish. It gives a lived feeling and adds a sense of time and history. Brand-new things are fine, but to me they reek of mass production. Give me an object that shows signs of a little age and I am a happy girl. If you can't wait for a well-used look to develop, you can hurry things along. Hang textiles outside for a week and the sunlight and weather will help to age them. Dye bright white fabrics with tea or coffee to soften their effect. To age a wood floor, have a dance party and ask your kids' friends to wear their sporty cleats. In no time, your floor will be distressed. Use a wire brush to distress a floor or piece of furniture quickly. A piece of furniture will become distressed if left outside for a few days, but beware—water can cause furniture to fall apart quickly and will wreck a finish that you want to retain.

I found a bookcase at a used-furniture store and had my contractor, Kevin, mount it on the wall to make a display piece for my pottery. On the shelves I have a mishmash of my own handmade pots, antique Mason's Ironstone, English transferware, and some contemporary potters' work. The vibrant colors all work together and create a happy still life. In the summer, I use the jugs for displaying flowers around our home.

kitchen we have another seating area we call "the daybed nook." In my opinion, every kitchen needs a daybed if there is space. It's a perfect spot to read, talk on the phone, or take a nap. I have piled the daybed with my hand-knit and hand-embroidered pillows and other pillows I have made out of molas, elaborate appliqué panels made by members of the Kuna tribe of Central America. I rotate an assortment of Indian bedspreads on the daybed as covers. I love that I can change the feeling of the nook by the season by doing something as simple as swapping covers! I adore the look of oil paintings but couldn't afford to purchase them, so I taught myself to paint with oils. Throughout the kitchen, I have old prints and my gouache paintings in frames I found at yard sales.

It's important to bring yourself into the design of a kitchen. Kitchen designers are great to work with, but unless you use your own ingenuity and add older pieces such as thrift shop treasures into your kitchen, you will end up with a kitchen that may look like everyone else's. Take the time and energy to collect things that will add that special something to your kitchen project. It may take a little longer, but you will have a spectacular room that you and your family will enjoy for years.

I keep most of our everyday dishes in my mother-in-law's corner cupboard. I love collecting dishes and pick them up at yard sales, flea markets, church sales, and antique stores and on visits to potters' studios. I even made some of them myself years back, when I made my own pottery. I have some sets of several of the same dish so that I can use one design to serve a group. I have many "onesies." They all seem to go together. It makes it more fun to have a variety instead of everything the same.

HOW TO MAKE
A DECORATIVE ARCHWAY

WHEN WE WERE REDOING THE KITCHEN, I SHOWED OUR CON-tractor, Kevin, a photo of a hall archway detail I loved from our previous home. That house was built in the 1880s and had some sweet Victorian touches. Kevin took one look at my photo and figured out how to build it into the hallway in our farmhouse. The new archway makes the transition from the kitchen to the living room, and the curved ceiling gives a bit of a Moroccan flair to the small hallway. It is one of those special details that can easily be added to a modern home that won't break the bank and brings a creative twist to a space.

1. Bend the Luan into the opening of your doorway and mark where the Luan meets the vertical door frame, creating an archway. Carefully cut the Luan using a table saw.

2. Using drywall screws, attach the Luan to the wall on both sides.

3. Using a piece of cardboard, trace the opening created by the curve. Repeat for other side. This pattern is used to cover the empty space between the arch and the door frame. Cut the pattern from the cardboard using a utility knife.

4. Cut the remaining Luan to match the cardboard pattern using a jigsaw.

5. Using glue, attach the cut Luan pieces to the wall and the new archway.

6. Cut 1 x 2-inch boards the length of the Luan. Nail in place, covering the bottom join of the archway to the wall.

7. Using plaster and a trowel, smooth a thin layer of plaster over the new archway. Once the plaster is dry, prime and paint the archway.

8. Using the air-dry clay, sculpt spiral flowers, leaves, and stems (see photograph). To make the flowers and the stems, roll the clay into a ½-inch "worm" as you did with modeling clay when you were a child. Form the "worm" into a spiral-shaped flower, beginning at the center. The flowers measure 3 inches in diameter when completely rolled. The flower stems are 5 inches long.

SUPPLIES

- 4 x 8-foot piece of Luan (a soft, very pliable type of plywood)
- Table saw
- Nails and drywall screws
- Cardboard, for pattern
- Wood filler
- Utility knife
- Jigsaw
- Carpenter's wood glue
- Two 1 x 2-inch boards the length of your hallway
- Plaster and trowel
- Primer
- Latex paint
- Air-dry modeling clay

To make the leaves, using your hands or a rolling pin, roll the clay ⅜ inch thick. Using a utility knife, cut leaf shapes out of the clay. Using your fingers and some water, smooth out the cut corners so that the leaf shapes are rounded. The leaves on the sides of the flowers are 4½ inches long. Additional decorative leaves are 2, 3½, and 4 inches long. You will need to customize your shapes to fit the space on your archway.

9. Let the flowers, stems, and leaves dry flat under plastic wrap to prevent warping. This can take a few days, depending on the humidity.

10. Using carpenter's glue, attach the clay flower pieces and leaves to the archway. If desired, paint the clay pieces in colors contrasting with the main base color.

SUPPLIES

- Scraps of brightly colored worsted-weight yarn
- Susan Bates pom pom maker, with mold sizes 1¼, 1¾, 2¼, and 3½ inches (see note)
- Scissors
- Tapestry needle
- 2 bells approximately 2 inches tall
- 1 bell 4 to 5 inches tall
- Hammer and 3 nails for hanging

A TORAN IS A TRADITIONAL HINDU DECORATIVE ORNAMENT that is hung over entrances in homes and at weddings and celebrations. Each person who walks through the doorway is blessed with good luck, happiness, and prosperity. Torans are often made of fabric and are heavily embroidered. At Indian wedding celebrations, torans are sometimes made from real marigolds.

Several years ago at an Indian import store I purchased three torans made from yellow, orange, red, and white fabrics, with dangling bells. At first I thought I would use them as Christmas decorations, but we liked the cheery look of them so much that we have kept them up for several years.

I am a big fan of pom poms made from scraps of yarn. I made my own version of a toran of yarn and three Indian bells. I hang our toran in our kitchen window.

NOTE: There are a number of pom pom makers on the market, and my preference is for the Susan Bates model, which has four mold sizes and results in very nice, even pom poms. Pom poms can also be made using a cardboard circle, although I prefer those from a mold.

{Continued}

1. Make the braid that the bell sections hang from. Cut 12 pieces of yarn of assorted colors into 72-inch lengths. Tie all 12 pieces of yarn together with an overhand knot about 3 inches from one end. Braid the yarn in typical fashion using 4 pieces of yarn in each of the three sections to make one big braid. Tie again to finish the braid at the end of the yarn.

2. Make multicolor pom poms (see "How to Make a Multicolor Pom Pom" on the next page). Make 14 pom poms with the 2¼-inch pom pom mold. Make 2 pom poms with the 3½-inch mold. Make 3 pom poms with the 1¼-inch mold.

3. Assemble the bell sections: 2 side sections and 1 center section. Thread together two 18-inch lengths of yarn on a tapestry needle. For the first side section, run the needle through 1 large pom pom, 1 medium pom pom, and 1 small pom pom, then through the smaller size bell hole, then back through the 3 pom poms. Tie the 2 ends together with an overhand knot and set aside. Do not trim the ends of the yarn. Make the second side bell section the same way.

   Make the center bell section the same way but use 2 medium-size pom poms and 1 small pom pom. Run your threaded tapestry needle through the larger bell hole, then back through the 3 pom poms. Tie the 2 ends together and set aside.

4. Measure the door or window opening you will be decorating to determine the exact length for the braid you made in step 1. My window is 35 inches wide, so I made my braid 47 inches long so it would form a nice curve. Beginning at one tied end of the braid, measure and then tie an overhand knot at the length you want. Cut the excess braid about 3 inches from the knot and loosen the braid to fringe the end.

5. Attach the bell sections. Using the yarn ends of the 2 bell sections, tie 1 of the side bell sections to the braid at each end. Tie the smaller bell section at the exact center of the braid. Cut the knots on the bell sections and thread ends of yarn into the pom poms and trim.

6. Attach the remaining pom poms to the braid section. Thread the pom pom tie ends through a needle and stitch the ends through to the back of the braid, spacing them evenly. Tie with a double overhand knot, weave ends into the pom poms, and trim.

7. To hang the toran, drive 3 nails into the window or door frame, 1 at each side and 1 in the middle. Drape the toran on the nails, pulling the center onto the middle nail.

HOW TO MAKE A MULTICOLOR POM POM

There are many ways to make a pom pom, but my favorite is to use a plastic pom pom maker. I prefer the Susan Bates brand, which comes with four sizes of pom pom "molds": 1¼, 1¾, 2¼, and 3½ inches. Using a pom pom maker is much more efficient than using a cardboard mold because you do not waste yarn when trimming, as you do with a cardboard mold. With a plastic mold, the yarn can also be more tightly packed (making these pom poms great kitty toys too). Follow the manufacturer's instructions that come with the pom pom maker.

One-color pom poms are fun on their own, but there are several methods for making multicolor pom poms.

For a random tweed effect, hold two or more colors together and wind them at the same time.

To make a patched effect, wind two light colors at the same time around one half of the mold, filling it halfway. Change colors and use two darker colors. Repeat for the second piece of the mold.

To make a random, multicolor pom pom, vary the colors as you wind. Pom poms eat yarn quickly, so they are a great way to work through your yarn stash.

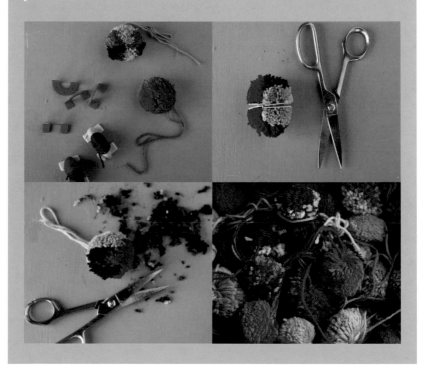

POTATO-PRINTED DISH TOWELS

TEXTILES ARE THE WORKHORSE OF THE KITCHEN, WHETHER they are colorful tablecloths, dishrags, pot holders, or dish towels. There is no need for items that work to be ugly. In fact, crafting textiles for use in your kitchen makes the daily cleaning work much more enjoyable. These brightly colored dish towels were printed with stamps made from three small fingerling potatoes. You could also make stamps of apples or pears. This is an easy project to do with kids, and it also makes a nice gift. If you really enjoy stamping, the entire dish towel could be covered with prints.

NOTE: For the dish towel, a smooth fabric is best. See the next section, "How to Make a Dish Towel," for instructions on making your own. When you use transparent textile paint, the fabric color affects the finished print color. I chose colors that were analogous to the dish towel color so that the print colors would be clear and bright. If I had chosen complementary colors, the shades would have canceled each other out and the print colors would have been drab. I printed with hot pink fabric paint on the orange towel, with bright green on the green towel, and with red on the yellow towel. On the white towel you can see each actual fabric paint color—hot pink, green, and red. Isn't it interesting to see how the base fabric color affects the printed outcome?

1. Cover your work surface with a dropcloth.
2. Using the ruler and the auto-fade marker, draw a horizontal line across the towel 3 inches from the bottom edge.
3. Cut each potato in half lengthwise. Rinse and dry the potatoes.
4. Using a foam paintbrush, dab the fabric paint onto the cut side of a potato. Press it onto the fabric placing the bottom edge of the potato on the marked line. Push firmly to transfer color to the dish towel. Continue across the line, varying the sizes and colors as you wish.
5. Following the manufacturer's directions, heat-set the fabric paint.

SUPPLIES

- Linen or cotton dish towels (see note)
- Dropcloth
- Graph ruler
- Auto-fade or vanishing fabric marker
- Fingerling potatoes, small, medium, and large
- Knife to cut potatoes
- 1-inch foam paintbrush
- Jacquard Textile Color in assorted colors (see note)
- Steam iron

HOW TO MAKE A DISH TOWEL

I make my own dish towels out of pure linen fabric. Most linen fabric is 54 inches wide. A standard dish towel size is 30 x 22 inches, so 1 yard of 54-inch-wide linen is enough for two dish towels. Cut 5 inches off the end of the linen to get a piece of fabric 31 inches long. Cut two dish towels, each one 23 x 31 inches. Turn the edge under 1/8 inch all the way around and press with a steam iron. Turn each side under 3/8 inch and press again. Using a sewing machine, sew along the folded edges, close to the fold.

STRIPED FELTED-WOOL
POT HOLDER

SUPPLIES

- Six 2 x 8-inch strips of felt fabric, in an assortment of colors (to make your own felt, see "How to Felt and Dye Wool," page 152)

- Pins

- Sewing machine or needle and thread

- 1 ceramic plate 7 inches in diameter (for circle template)

- Auto-fade or vanishing fabric marker

- 1 piece of backing felt approximately 7 inches square

- Scissors

WOOL FELT MAKES THE MOST AMAZING AND USEFUL POT holders. The wool fabric will not burn and it is a great insulator. Once you begin using these pot holders, you will throw away all your flammable cotton ones. These are a great use for homemade felt and for taking care of odds and ends of felted sweaters. Commercial felt works, too, although it is not as thick. Felt pot holders can be washed in the washing machine because the felted wool has already shrunk. The instructions below are for a round pot holder.

1. Assemble the front of the pot holder. Lay one felt strip over another with an overlap of ⅜ inch and pin the strips together. Sew them together ¼ inch from the edge of the top strip. Repeat with the 4 other strips until all 6 strips are sewn together. (See illustration.)

2. Using the plate and the auto-fade marker, trace a circle on the wrong side of the backing felt. Cut out the circle. Lay it wrong side down on the backside of the felt strips and pin. (See illustration.)

3. With the backing circle facing up, sew through the 2 layers ¼ inch from the edge. Trim the pot holder close to your stitching through all the layers.

Step 1

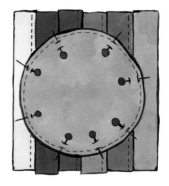

Step 2

SHEPHERD'S PIE

One of our favorite family meals is shepherd's pie made with ground lamb from our flock of sheep. It's an easy recipe to prepare ahead, freezes well, and makes nice leftovers. It's yummy and homey and will feed a crowd. If you don't eat lamb, you can substitute lentils, ground beef, or ground turkey.

Preheat oven to 375 degrees. Peel and chop the potatoes. Boil in salted water until tender and mashable. Drain. Add the milk and butter. Mash the potatoes, season to taste with salt and pepper, and set aside.

Brown the lamb. Drain fat and set lamb aside in a separate bowl. In the same pan, sauté the onions and garlic in the olive oil on medium-low heat until onions are translucent, taking care not to burn the garlic! Add the diced carrots and sauté for 3 more minutes. Mix the broth, stock or wine, tomato paste, herbs, and salt and pepper together. Add this mixture and the ground lamb to the skillet and simmer until carrots are done to your liking. The mixture should be thick. If too saucy, simmer to let some of the moisture evaporate. Add the peas and corn if you are using them.

Butter a 9 x 13-inch casserole. Pour in the meat mixture and smooth. Spoon the potatoes over the top of the meat and spread evenly. Bake for 30 to 40 minutes, or until the casserole is bubbling. Sprinkle with parmesan cheese. Broil to melt the cheese and brown the top. Let stand for 5 minutes before serving.

INGREDIENTS

2 pounds potatoes

1 cup milk

2 tablespoons butter

1 pound ground lamb

1 tablespoon olive oil

1 onion, diced

2 carrots, diced into ½-inch pieces

5 cloves garlic, minced

1 cup chicken broth, lamb stock, or white wine

1 tablespoon tomato paste

½ teaspoon dried rosemary

½ teaspoon dried thyme

Salt and pepper

1 cup each corn and peas, fresh or frozen (optional)

¼ cup parmesan cheese

CH. 4

THE

PORCH

AS WE LIVED IN OUR FARMHOUSE FOR A FEW YEARS, WE found we didn't use the original porch, which was off the cellar kitchen. It was a nice space, but it was difficult to bring food and dishes down the winding staircase. I began to think about how to change the structure of our house and came up with a plan to add a second level to the original porch. In 2010, with permits in hand, we constructed a porch off the kitchen and the new studio below it, where the original porch had been.

Every region in the country has vernacular architecture—buildings that are traditional to the area they are built in. In New England, there is a tradition of the rambling farmhouse, often with an attached barn. My goal was to have the new porch/studio addition look like it wasn't new. This is hard to do, but I envisioned the addition looking like an old barn that had been retrofitted as living space. I used untreated pine vertical exterior siding that is typically found on New England barns and weathers to a lovely gray. We chose to bring the outside in with large casement windows for lots of natural light.

The new porch is a great space for watching the sheep graze while drinking coffee in the morning or hanging out for an afternoon on the wicker furniture. I wanted the walls to be a backdrop for the seasonal changes to the scenery outside, so I chose to paint the horizontally mounted pine boards with old-fashioned whitewash stain. As time goes on, the knots and grain will become more prominent and the texture will add to the old-fashioned feeling. The ceiling is made of V-groove pine boards, which I protected with exterior spar varnish. They will darken with time.

A screened-in porch is one of the greatest pleasures a homeowner can have. To be inside (away from the mosquitoes) but feel like you are outside is such a luxury. Porches are all about comfort, about whiling away the hours and escaping the heat. The wicker furniture is covered with a constantly rotating selection of Indian bedspreads. I have been decorating with Indian bedspreads—sometimes called Indian tapestries and often found in college dormitories—for years. Their colors and patterns always seem to match each other and fit into the ethnic textile and color theme of our home. I wrap them tightly around the cushions and tuck the excess fabric underneath. They work great for a house that has heavy traffic and lots of animals, as they can be removed quickly and laundered. The sun has faded their colors, which adds to their charm.

Our home has become the land of cast-off furniture. The different tables, chairs, and stools have all been donated by family members or picked up from the side of the road. I have painted the many tables and chairs in fun colors to create a party atmosphere. I have a colorful hand-woven antique kilim rug on the floor and handmade and embroidered pillows in bright colors on the furniture.

An addition like our porch-studio was an expensive project, and we thought long and hard about whether we could afford the cost. We had to weigh the benefits of the added space against the cost of the project. Because we didn't plan on moving anytime in the near future, we decided to spend the money. We are really happy we did, because the space has become our favorite room in the summer for breakfast, lunch, and dinner. Sometimes decisions have to be made that may not make total financial sense but do make a home more enjoyable to live in. The nicest feature (and the biggest money splurge) was the large windows. Old farm-houses have very little light and small windows. The new room really brings the outside weather and atmosphere into our home. It's a bonus that we can watch our sheep graze and see the colors of the mountain change with the seasons. In order for the ideas in my head to become a reality, I had a local woman who had archi-tectural drawing expertise do measured plans off of my sketches. Our contractor could then take her exact drawings and use them as his guide. The properly drawn plans also made me feel better about ordering the large number of windows— knowing that I would be getting the correct size.

Old chairs have such character, often possessing fancily shaped spindles and rails, but they can be rickety. I sometimes find them by the side of the road. I always wiggle them and sit in them before taking them to make sure they won't be too much work for me or end up in the bonfire burn pile. Oak office chairs make great dining table chairs. They are very sturdy and can be repainted in bright colors. I use enamel paints so the chairs can be easily washed.

HOW TO MAKE A STAMP FOR PRINTING FABRIC AND WALLS

THIS HAS GOT TO BE ONE OF THE SIMPLEST PROJECTS I have ever tried, and it results in a most sophisticated-looking end product. With some kids' fun foam, grayboard foam insulation from the lumberyard, and some latex paint, you can print any flat surface—walls, paper, floors, and fabric. The end result is perfect with its imperfectness, for it carries the mark of the printer's hand. It is also a fun project to do with children.

1. To make the stamp, enlarge the template as given or draw your own motif (see "How to Make Your Own Motifs and Patterns," page 86). Cut out the paper template. Using tape, attach it to a piece of fun foam with adhesive backing. Cut the motif out of the fun foam.

2. Remove the paper from the adhesive backing of the foam and push firmly to stick the foam template to your foam insulation or acrylic mount.

3. For uses when exact pattern registration is not necessary, use builder's foam insulation for your mount. To trim the insulation board close to the stamping motif, use a sharp utility knife and make a shallow cut around the motif. Gently snap the foam and it will break along the cut.

4. For uses where you need to see where you are stamping, as for a complex floral design, mount your foam stamp on an acrylic see-through mount. You can have these made at glass supply stores or purchase them online. In a pinch, a clear CD jewel case will work too.

SUPPLIES

- Kids' fun foam with adhesive backing
- Motif template (see "Templates" section, page 192, or make your own motif)
- Scissors
- Tape
- 1-inch foam insulation board (available at building supply stores in 4 x 8-foot sheets)
- Acrylic see-through stamp mounts (optional)
- Utility knife

TIPS FOR SUCCESSFUL STAMPING

1. Have some water available to rinse foam brushes and a sponge to wash stamps when you change colors.
2. Practice stamping first: on scraps of cloth when you are fabric printing or on cardboard boxes when you are printing on walls.
3. An apron or smock will keep you neat.
4. A hair dryer is handy for quicker drying. When printing fabric, it is best to let the paint dry naturally.
5. Use rags to wipe off mistakes when you are printing floors and walls. It is impossible to remove printing mistakes from fabric.

HOW TO MAKE YOUR OWN MOTIFS AND PATTERNS

THERE IS SOMETHING INCREDIBLY SATISFYING ABOUT designing your own motifs and patterns. Even if it is similar to a design someone else has come up with in the past, the simple act of making a motif yourself will have you feeling like a design rock star. Once you begin designing your own motifs and patterns, you will realize that your home is your own to transform into your very own patterned masterpiece. You can decorate wrapping paper, fabric, tabletops, walls, floors, ceilings, and more all with your very own designs.

MAKING MOTIFS

A motif is a single design. Motifs can be as simple as a repeating square or a line, or be more intricate such as ferns, leaves, and flowers. I have provided a number of motifs for the projects in this book (see "Templates" section, page 191), but it's easy to make your own.

To begin, choose a geometric shape to be your first motif. They are easy to draw and fun to print. Stripes, plaids, gingham checks, polka dots, chevrons, twills, and diagonal lines are all considered motifs and become a pattern.

You will find ideas for motifs everywhere you look. Walk outside and pick up some leaves and flowers. Open a magazine and look at the patterns on the rugs, the sofas, the walls. They are full of motifs. Individual letters, office equipment, telephones, bits of packaging—everywhere you look, you will find ideas for design motifs. The hard part is to break down all you see and choose a single object to be your motif.

One of the easiest ways to design your own motifs is by folding paper and then cutting a shape. This is how I designed almost all the motifs I used for the patterns I have printed.

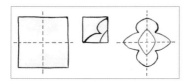

Figure 1

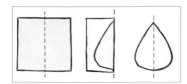

Figure 2

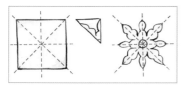

Figure 3

TWO-PART MOTIF: Fold a square piece of paper in half and cut half a leaf shape. It will be a mirror image. (See Figure 1.)

FOUR-PART MOTIF: Fold a square piece of paper in half, then in half again to make a square. Cut a shape from it and it will be mirrored 4 ways. (See Figure 2.)

EIGHT-PART MOTIF: Fold a square piece of paper in half, then in half again to make a square, then fold the paper on the diagonal. Cut a shape and it will be symmetrical 8 ways. (See Figure 3.)

Create all kinds of motifs by cutting folded paper and seeing what happens. Trust me, it is hard to stop! Once you like your shapes, turn them into stamps for creating one-of-a-kind details on walls or fabrics.

MAKING PATTERNS

Figure 4

Repeating a single motif or set of motifs is what makes a pattern. Most of my printed designs are free-form and random and do not follow a repetitive pattern. Overall though, they create their own kind of random pattern by mixing the same motifs to make a whole. If you are a more orderly person and prefer making a pattern repeat, there are two main types: side repeat and drop repeat.

SIDE REPEAT: This type of repeat is completely symmetrical. The same motif will be evenly spaced next to, above, and below one another producing a design that follows a grid. (See Figure 4.)

DROP REPEAT: A drop repeat moves every other vertical column of motifs halfway down creating a shifted pattern. (See Figure 5.)

Figure 5

HANGING EMBROIDERY HOOP "LANTERNS"

SUPPLIES

• 2 wood embroidery hoops of the same size (each hoop consists of two nested hoops)

• Fabric remnants

• Sewing machine or needle and thread

• Craft glue

• Small craft paintbrush for glue

FOR MANY YEARS, I HAD BRIGHTLY COLORED CHINESE PAPER lanterns hanging over the porch table to create a festive atmosphere. They finally shredded and disintegrated, so I replaced them with homemade "lanterns" made out of my cherished ethnic fabric remnants. These hanging lanterns would also make great outdoor decorations. Use little Christmas tree lights to illuminate them if you have electricity handy.

1. Measure the outside circumference of the inner ring of the embroidery hoop.

2. Cut a piece of fabric with one edge the same size as the circumference plus 1 inch and the other edge as long as you want the lantern. I made many lengths from 8 to 12 inches long.

3. Fold the fabric in half with the wrong side out, aligning the lengthwise edges. Sew a seam ½ inch from the edge to make a fabric tube. Turn the fabric tube right side out and press.

4. Using craft glue and brush, paint some glue around the outer edge of the inner hoop.

5. Stretch the seamed fabric tube around the hoop, lining it up so that the fabric edge is flush with one edge of the hoop. Place the outer piece of the hoop over the fabric and tighten it.

6. Repeat for the bottom hoop, rotating the screw fastener 180 degrees opposite the top one so that it will balance the weight.

7. Make a "handle" for the lantern. Thread a needle with a 36-inch length of thread. Double the thread and knot it. Stitch the thread to one side of the top of the lantern, then to the opposite side.

8. Hang and enjoy.

PAINTED COFFEE TABLE

FURNITURE THAT HAS SEEN BETTER DAYS CAN BE UPDATED with paint. It is fun to paint a design on a tabletop—it will act as a tablecloth and always be a bright spot in a room. The coffee table I painted originally had a glass top, which I broke. I had a piece of ¾-inch plywood cut at the home store, rounded the corners with a jigsaw, and then painted it in this simple but colorful design made of overlapping circles. The circles were drawn onto the table by using plates, bowls, and glasses as templates. Designing doesn't have to be hard. Look around your home to see what objects you can use as templates.

1. Remove any loose or flaking paint on your table with a putty knife. Sand the tabletop to prepare for painting.

2. Prime the tabletop. If you are painting on raw wood, prime it twice.

3. Paint the base coat. If it hasn't covered thoroughly, paint it a second time.

4. Trace very lightly around the outside of different-size templates with a pencil. Space the circles out around the tabletop so that they are aesthetically pleasing to your eye. Where the circles overlap, draw very lightly so that the pencil marks will not show through.

5. Using small artist brushes, begin painting the circles with the colors you have chosen. Where the circles overlap, decide on the color you are going to use on top. Some of the circles will need to be "cut in" with a smaller artist's brush. Continue painting until the colors look good. Some colors will need more layers of paint than others.

6. When you are happy with how the table looks, let the paint dry thoroughly. Then paint it with the spar varnish. I applied three coats so that the surface will be water-resistant and very durable.

SUPPLIES

- Wooden table
- Putty knife
- 150 grit sandpaper
- Primer
- Latex paint in turquoise, gold, topaz, brown, cinnamon, geranium red, orange, chartreuse, olive green, dark teal, and bisque
- 1½-inch paintbrush and artist's brushes in an assortment of sizes
- Pencil
- Assorted round shapes for templates such as glasses, bowls, plates, and deli containers
- Spar varnish
- China bristle brush for spar varnish
- Paint thinner to clean brush

PAISLEY-STAMPED TABLECLOTH

THE PAISLEY MOTIF IS ONE OF MY FAVORITES OF ALL TIME.
The organic shape reminds me of a pear or a kidney bean. It decorated
many of the print fabrics I made my clothing from when I was a teen. Later
I learned about the amazing history of the paisley motif. It originated in In-
dia and Iran and is commonly seen on all kinds of textile designs from these
regions. When textiles traveled the Silk Route and came into Europe, many
European makers adopted the motif for print, woven, and embroidered deco-
ration. The word paisley *comes from the Scottish town where intricately pat-*
terned woven shawls were made on handlooms rigged to weave up to fifteen
colors at a time. The simple asymmetrical shape combines nicely with other
organic motifs such as flowers and leaves, like those you see on my stamped
tablecloth.

NOTE: For this project I prefer using latex paint with a fabric medium rather than fabric paint. The latex paint is more opaque than fabric paints, and once you have bought a selection of small sample jars of paint, it's considerably cheaper. For this project I used brown, ultramarine blue, geranium, orange, light turquoise, dark teal, green, and gold. The fabric medium I used was Golden GAC-900. I used 4 yards of 72-inch-wide fabric (Dharma Trading's PFD, "prepped for dyeing") to create a tablecloth that measured 120 x 68 inches when finished. To make a tablecloth to fit your table, you will need fabric that is wider than your table. For the length you need as many feet as your table is long, plus 2 feet for overhang. Take into consideration shrinkage when purchasing fabric. My fabric shrank 17 percent in length but not much in width.

SUPPLIES

- Templates A–I (see "Templates" section, page 193)
- Kids' fun foam with adhesive backing for making stamps
- 1-inch-thick foam building insulation (often called gray or blue board)
- Scissors
- Tape
- Utility knife
- Pencil with new eraser
- 3 wine corks
- Rubber band
- ⅜-inch dauber or larger pencil with new eraser (to print decorative dots)

FOR THE TABLECLOTH

- 100 percent cotton canvas (see note)
- Sewing machine
- Steam iron
- Dropcloth
- Latex paint in an assortment of colors (see note)
- Fabric medium to soften dried paint (see note)
- 1-inch foam brush

- Deli containers with lids for mixing fabric paint
- Large table for printing
- Fabric and craft scissors

1. Prewash your fabric and dry it in the dryer. Remove it before it is completely dry so the wrinkles don't set.

2. Hem the edges. Turn the fabric under ¼ inch and press, then turn it under again ½ inch and press again. Sew with matching-color thread.

3. Prepare your stamps. Referring to the instructions on "How to Make a Stamp for Printing Fabric and Walls" on page 84, make stamps using templates A–I. You'll also be using the eraser end of the pencil and the wine corks for stamping. To make the 3 circle stamp, hold 3 wine corks together and fasten with a rubber band.

{Continued}

4. Cover your work surface with a dropcloth. Wrinkles in the dropcloth will affect the stamped designs, so be sure to smooth it out.

5. Mix the latex paint with the fabric medium, following the manufacturer's directions. You don't need a lot of paint. If you run out, you can always mix more. I begin by mixing just 1 tablespoon of paint with the recommended amount of fabric medium.

6. Use the foam brush to apply paint to your stamp. Press the stamp firmly onto the fabric. Try a few sample stamps on some scraps of fabric to get the feeling. Begin to stamp your pattern by working in just one section of the tablecloth. Refer to the photo or create your own pattern. When changing colors, wash the stamp with water to remove previous color. As you begin stamping and mixing the different colors and stamps, your pattern will build with each motif added. If you're creating your own pattern and you want your tablecloth to be symmetrical at either end, print one end first. Then print the opposite end matching the motifs and colors in placement. To make it easier, take a photo of the first end, print the photo, then duplicate the design on the other end of the fabric. Work the center section last, filling in the middle area with an interesting pattern, keeping in mind that you may want a center focus for the design. Let each section dry overnight before moving onto the next section of the cloth. My tablecloth took parts of 3 days—a day for each end and a third day for the middle section.

7. Heat-set the paint on the tablecloth, following the fabric medium manufacturer's recommendation.

SCOTT'S HAND-STAMPED ROCKING CHAIR PAD

THE OLD ROCKING CHAIR ON OUR PORCH CAME FROM THE home of a dear friend of mine named Scott. When he passed away, I was given one of the chairs that had sat on his porch. It was a lovely shade of turquoise but was in need of a seat repair. When I took the worn seat off, I discovered a hand-woven rush seat that had been patched with plywood. Instead of getting too involved in carpentry, I made a chair cushion out of hand-printed fabric. Unlike the Paisley-Stamped Tablecloth, this project uses motifs that are layered on top of each other. In order to see where to print the second layer on the flowers, use acrylic mounts, in place of the foam building insulation, when making your stamps. The see-through acrylic square can be cut at glass shops, or clear jewel cases for CDs work, too. The sewn chair pads are sized to fit a standard chair seat. I have lots of different vintage chairs in our home, and this size fits them all.

NOTE: For the stamps I used acrylic blocks for mounting all but template A, which I mounted on builder's foam insulation board. For the canvas I used Dharma Trading's PFD "prepped for dyeing" fabric.

1. Prepare your stamps. Referring to the instructions on "How to Make a Stamp for Printing Fabric and Walls" on page 84, make stamps using templates A–C. You'll also be using the wine cork and pencil eraser as a stamp.
2. Iron your fabric. Cover your printing surface with a dropcloth.
3. Mix your paint colors with the fabric medium. You will not need much paint for this project. I began with one tablespoon of paint mixed with the recommended amount of fabric medium.
4. Using a foam brush and stamp A, dab the paint onto the foam that is mounted on your block. You do not need much paint, just a thin coating. Press firmly onto the fabric. Do a few practice stamps on scrap fabric to get the feeling and the amount of pressure needed. Continue using stamp A to print the

SUPPLIES

FOR THE STAMPS

- Templates A–C (see "Templates" section, page 196)
- Kids' fun foam with adhesive backing
- Acrylic mounts (see note)
- 1-inch-thick foam building insulation (often called gray or blue board)
- Scissors
- Tape
- Utility knife
- Wine cork
- Pencil with fresh eraser end

FOR THE CHAIR PAD

- ⅔ yard 100 percent cotton canvas (see note)
- Latex paint in fuchsia, watermelon, purple, green, and bright turquoise
- Golden GAC 900 fabric medium
- Dropcloth
- 1-inch foam brush
- Deli containers with lids for mixing fabric paint

- Chair pad template (see "Templates" section, page 195)
- 16-inch-square down pillow insert, or ½ yard of 1-inch-thick foam and polyfill stuffing (for stuffing corners if not using down pillow insert)
- Sewing machine
- Hand sewing needle
- Thread
- Iron
- Pins and fabric scissors
- Steam iron

fabric overall with the design, alternating between colors (I used fuchsia and watermelon) and spacing the flower designs approximately 2 to 4 inches apart. Leave room for the leaves. Let dry.

5. Use stamp B to print the flower petals. Using the color of your choice (I used purple), stamp each flower background with the flower detail.

6. Use stamp C to print 3 leaves around each flower. I used green.

7. Use the wine cork to print the centers of flowers. I used bright turquoise.

{Continued}

8. Use the eraser end of a pencil to fill the empty spaces of the fabric with polka dots. I used bright turquoise.

9. Heat-set the fabric following the manufacturer's instructions.

10. Iron the fabric and fold it in half with selvage edges aligned. Pin the template for the chair cushion to the fabric. Cut the template through the two layers of fabric.

11. Cut 4 pieces of fabric 2½ inches wide by 12 inches long to be used as chair ties.

12. For each piece of chair tie fabric, fold the fabric under to the wrong side by ¼ inch on each long side. Press with an iron. Fold the ties in half lengthwise, wrong sides together, aligning the two folded edges. Pin along the vertical edge and sew close to the edge. (See illustration.)

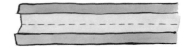

Step 12

13. Pin two ties next to each other at each rounded corner of one of the chair pad pieces. Baste in place and remove pins. Clip the loose ends of the ties on the diagonal to prevent fraying. (See illustration.)

14. Pin the two chair pad pieces together with right sides facing. Sew around the chair pad, ½ inch from the edge leaving a 10-inch opening at the back between the two sets of ties. Clip notches at the rounded corners and clip the two sharp corners. Turn right side out through the opening in the back.

Step 13

15. Trim the foam pad to be the same size of the finished cover. Insert into the cover. If using a down pillow, place it into the chair pad. Stuff the corners with polyfill so that the entire chair pad is firm. Sew the opening closed.

DOWN PILLOW INSERTS

Did you know that if you use a down pillow insert larger than the size of your pillow or chair pad case, the pillow will look puffier and be fuller? Down inserts last for years and they don't get lumpy like polyfill inserts. They can be washed in any washing machine. Put them in the dryer with a tennis ball to make sure the down dries fluffy and lofted, not matted together.

BRING IN FRESH FLOWERS

During the growing season, I like to bring the outside in. In the spring that means branches from flowering shrubs and perennial flowers. In the summer, I have vases of zinnias, amaranth, wildflowers, and annuals. In the fall, large bounteous sunflowers fill the jugs. As the leaves turn, I find colorful branches for my flower arrangements. It is fun to use odd wild plants such as vines and fruiting shrubs to add interest to arrangements.

Cut flowers early in the morning or late in the day. Remove all the green leaves that will be below the waterline. I do this outside so the leaves can easily be added to the compost pile. When cutting sunflowers, cut them before the blooms are rounded and mature. They will continue to develop in a vase. Keep your arrangements out of direct sun as the heat will quicken their decline.

To make flowers last longer, always wash the vase between uses to rid it of any bacteria. Although florists advise changing the water frequently, I never have time for that. A quarter teaspoon of liquid bleach will help the flowers last a bit longer. Fact is—they have been cut and are going to die, but they sure do make a room feel more cheerful.

CH. 5

THE

LIVING ROOM

A LIVING ROOM SHOULD BE A SPACE FOR LIVING THAT IS
warm and inviting—a room you want to stay in for hours. Our living room is the
largest room in our house and the space we use for entertaining, family parties,
and relaxing in the winter in front of a roaring fire. In the early days of the farmhouse, this room would have been the kitchen, bedroom, and "everything" room.
It features a huge fireplace, and to the right of the fireplace is a domed bread oven
that I use for making pizza. Most farmhouses built around the same time as ours
had huge central chimneys that functioned as a heat source and a cooking space.
Not many such fireplaces and chimneys still remain because of the amount of
space they take up on all floors of a house.

Our living room is rectangular and very long. I chose colors and decorating
accessories that would make the room feel warm, cozy, and smaller. I also split the
furniture groupings so that there would be different areas in the room—a hallway,
seating area, and library area. By using many colors, I was able to give the room a
lived-in feeling, as if our family had been here many decades.

A quick way to make a stunning picture display is to frame the pages of an old book or a reprint of an antique book. Favorite books of mine are Owen Jones's Grammar of Ornament *and Albertus Seba's* Cabinet of Natural Curiosities. *Used bookstores, library book sales, and eBay are great places to find decorative old books.*

I chose a palette of analogous colors to make the room feel warm and chose to paint some of the walls with easy decorative paint techniques. The decorative painting gives the room a handmade feeling. It is amazing how a color or colors can stay with you in your visual memory for years. I began on the north side of the room by colorwashing the walls—layering paint colors and then wiping a colorwash over them—to look like a gold I had seen on a trip to Italy, which I call Tuscan gold. The Tuscan gold color was created by layering analogous colors randomly on top of a light yellow base. I finished with a thin wash of orangey gold (see "How to Colorwash a Wall," page 177). I trimmed the Tuscan gold walls with an olive green stamped border inspired by my collection of Indian textiles. The resulting design has a very charming handmade look.

The south and east walls are covered with wood paneling. I painted them with an easy decorative paint technique called dragging, which resulted in a lovely streaky chartreuse color (see "How to Paint a Dragged Wall," page 112). Combining these three different decorative painting techniques gives a feeling of unplanned serendipity.

The west wall consists of a room-wide bookcase and cabinet unit painted a bright olive green. Throughout the room I used shades of green—aqua, moss, bright green, and olive green—for the doors and window trim. Although it may seem chaotic, in fact, using related shades holds a space together.

Books make any room look cozy and serve as part of this room's décor. Over the years we have collected many textile, art, and animal husbandry titles, which we refer to again and again. In front of the bookcase is a "library table," which holds more books and the office typewriter that my dad used to type me notes when I was at college. I get a kick out of the little kids who visit and have never seen a typewriter before. Choosing accessories that may not be current but have an interesting history can start many a conversation.

When I think of the standard living room, it conjures up for me the phrase "best room in the house." Many people don't use their living rooms very often, and I think that is a shame. Often, the furniture is off-limits to kids and animals, and there is an aura of do not touch. I wanted our living room to be anything but. The furniture is mostly well-made wood antiques of different vintages and styles. A favorite piece is the Indian carved chest inlaid with shells that serves as a coffee table in front of the fireplace. I am in the camp of not ever wanting to paint or refinish really old furniture if it has a great patina, yet I do love the casual look of painted furniture. Although it is difficult to determine what furniture may have future

value, I use the hundred-year standard. Any furniture less than a hundred years old is ripe for painting. Along one of the chartreuse walls, I painted my Aunt Jen's oak sideboard a glossy bright red. I love how the complementary colors bounce off each other.

The fabrics on the comfortable chairs and sofa are jacquard weaves, meaning that the design is woven into the fabric, making it a good choice for upholstered coverings that need to be long-wearing. On all of the furniture I use layers of ethnic, plaid, and patterned textiles in the form of wool and mohair throws and my handmade pillows. Our house is chilly and drafty, and having a warm, pretty throw on each seat is very functional. If you live in an area where it is warmer, look for cotton and lightweight throws. The floors are covered with Persian and Oriental rugs hand-woven in a slew of colorful designs. They anchor the room with their warm colors and rectangular shapes.

Early period homes do not have overhead lights, which can make their rooms a bit dark and depressing. Because we do a lot of reading in this room, I have had to find plenty of floor and table lamps. I've added color and pattern to many of the lamps by painting the shades with fabric paints and designs. They make the room look cheerful and create another layer of warmth with their glow.

Creating a room such as this takes years to build the layers, the colors, the experiences, and the ambience. Any home takes time, so be patient and let it all grow organically as you create your home. A living room is a perfect place to display personal collections. It is fun to choose a theme and build on it for several decades. Collections can be centered on a hobby or a career or a passion. As sheep farmers, we have collected all kinds of sheep-y items, including wood engravings, which are hung on one living room wall, and antique British sheep ceramics. Perhaps you are a musician. Framed antique sheet music is truly beautiful. Are you a writer? Why not frame old letters found at flea markets. Traveler? How about vintage postcards of places you have been. It's all about adding your personality and a bit of quirkiness to make your home a personal statement.

When you are designing your home, try to think of things that are important in your life that you would like to build collections on or base a room around. There is no need to build a collection quickly. It makes it more fun to spread collecting out over the years so you always have something to be on the lookout for. Objects should tell a story, so be ready to share the story of your home and the objects in it with your guests—your collection will help to get conversations flowing and will also show your guests what you and your family are about.

HOW TO PAINT A DRAGGED WALL

SUPPLIES

DRAGGING IS A TRADITIONAL METHOD OF DECORATIVE painting that works particularly well on woodwork and trim. It is created by painting a base coat in a light color and then lightly dragging a second color over the first coat to make a streaky effect. I used yellow for the base coat and olive green for the dragging coat. The second color is thinned to make it "drag" more effectively. We have a lot of wood paneling in our home, and I chose the dragging technique because the lines of the vertical boards supply a guide for the paintbrush to slide along. I have also done dragging on furniture, with great success. You need to work quickly because the thinned paint will dry quickly. If you make a mistake, it can be rubbed off with a rag immediately. As with all decorative painting techniques, you might want to experiment and practice on a board or the inside of a closet door. Different paintbrushes will give different effects. I use an inexpensive regular paintbrush to create the dragged effect, but there are special decorative painting brushes called dragging brushes designed especially for this technique.

Dragging can be done with both oil-based and latex paint, but since working with latex paint is simpler than with oil, I give instructions here for latex. Painting a layer of sealant will help protect the dragged paint from wear that may occur as a result of the slight texture of the topcoat.

- Semi-gloss latex paint in two colors (a lighter shade for the base and a darker analogous shade for the dragging color)
- Dropcloth
- Paintbrushes
- Inexpensive 4-inch paintbrush, for dragging
- Plastic bucket
- Rags
- Polyurethane (optional)

1. Paint your surface with the base color. I used a light yellow color. It is best to choose a light color for your base coat. It will show through the top streaky layer adding a second layer of color to the walls. Be sure it is completely dry before going on to the next step.

2. Use water to thin the second color to the consistency of cream.

3. Dip the dragging brush into your paint, then remove most of the paint by brushing it on the inside of the container. Beginning at the top of the wall, pull the paintbrush down the wall, creating a streaky ribbon of paint. Make sure

the paint is applied thinly to avoid creating drips that will look messy. The base color should show through.

4. When your brush runs out of paint, reload it with the dragging color. Feather the new paint on the brush into the dragged paint already on the wall. If the join looks uneven, go back and feather the join again. Be careful at this point, because the more paint you add, the darker and more noticeable the join will become. As you work your way around the room, make the feathering points at different heights so that they won't be noticeable.

5. Work fast, for the paint dries quickly. If you make a mistake, wipe the paint off immediately with a rag and try again.

6. Cover the dry dragged wall with a protective coat of polyurethane.

CROCHETED AFGHAN
OF MOD GRANNY SQUARES

SUPPLIES

• Color By Kristin yarn by Classic
Elite Yarns (50% Wool, 25%
Mohair, 25% Alpaca; 93 yards /
50 grams): 25 balls in 8 colors
as follows:

    4 balls of Geranium 3258

    3 balls Lichen 3281

    3 balls Lady's Mantle 3235

    3 balls Deep Blue Sea 3248

    3 balls Aubergine 3226

    2 balls October Leaves 3278

    3 balls Raspberry 3232

    4 balls Yarrow 3243

• Size H crochet hook

• Tapestry needle for sewing
squares together

GAUGE

Each square will measure
approximately 12 inches when
blocked.

ABBREVIATIONS

Ch—chain

Dc—double crochet

St(s)—Stitch(es)

</>—indicates corner stitches

*THE ART OF CROCHET HAS LONG BEEN ASSOCIATED WITH
grannies. Although the social implications may not be what modern crocheters want to hear, I think the tradition of grandmothers teaching younger
people to crochet is one of the most special ways anyone can share their craft
with a new stitcher. I was taught to crochet by my grandmother Frieda.
She came to this country from Germany in 1910 and brought with her a
rich family history of needlework. Gram was always making something—
whether quilting, sewing, baking, crocheting, arranging flowers. She often
said, "Idle hands do the devil's work."*

*Traditional crocheted granny squares made into afghans are one of the
most popular projects to make. They are quick to do, the stitch pattern is
easily memorized, and the color combinations are endless. For this Afghan
of Mod Granny Squares I worked the rich colors in a graphic fashion so that
the bold square-in-square motif plays upon the colors. It is a lacey, warm,
and colorful afghan that drapes beautifully and is awesome to snuggle under. You can easily adjust the colors to fit your décor.*

FINISHED SIZE: 48 X 60 INCHES

Make 20 mod granny squares. Each square begins with 1 color that is worked for
4 rounds. The second color is added and worked for the remainder of the square.
Follow the chart provided for color placement and sewing together.

MOD GRANNY SQUARE

With center color ch4. Join into a round with a slip st at the beg of the chain.

Round 1: Ch3 (this will act as the first dc and you will join it with the end of
the round), 2 dc, ch2, (3 dc, ch2) 3 times, slip st to join to the 3rd chain
stitch from foundation chain.

{Continued}

Color A Geranium 3258

Color B Lichen 3281

Color C Lady's Mantle 3235

Color D Deep Blue Sea 3248

Color E Aubergine 3226

Color F October Leaves 3278

Color G Raspberry 3232

Color H Yarrow 3243

Color Chart

Round 2: Ch3, 2 dc in the space below where chain come out of, ch2, (3 dc, ch2, 3 dc to form corner, ch2) 3 times, 3 dc in space, ch2, slip st to join to the 3rd chain stitch you crocheted at the beginning of the round.

Round 3: Ch3, 2 dc in space below that chain came out of, (ch2, <3 dc in next space, 3 dc, ch2, 3 dc to form corner>) 3 times, ch2, 3 dc, ch2, 3 dc, ch2, slip st to join to the 3rd chain stitch you worked at the beginning of the round.

Round 4: Ch3, 2 dc in space below that chain came out of, (ch2, 3 dc into space, ch2, 3 dc into space, ch2, <3 dc in next space, 3 dc, ch2, 3 dc to form corner>) 3 times, 3 dc in space, ch2, slip st to join to the 3rd chain stitch you worked at the beginning of the round. Break center color yarn.

Round 5: Join outer square color yarn with a slip knot into any corner st. Continue as before working 3 dc into each open space with 2 chains on each side and working corner stitches as before.

Square is complete when you have worked a total of 10 rounds: 4 in the center color and 6 in the outer color.

FINISHING

Using a whipstitch (see illustration), stitch the squares together using the darker color at each join and seam.

WHIPSTITCH: Join the yarn in the corner of a square by taking 2 small stitches on the back of one of the loops. Begin joining two squares together with overhand stitching. Use the darker color of yarn when joining squares.

POM POM APPLIQUÉ PILLOW

PILLOWS ARE AN EASY WAY TO ADD COLOR ACCENTS TO A room. A handmade pillow makes a statement that your home is a place full of creativity and warmth. I have made many different kinds of pillows to decorate our home over the years—some sewn, some embroidered, some knit. This Pom Pom Appliqué Pillow uses simple appliqué with felt fabric. The flower shapes are hand-stitched to the pillowcase with easy embroidery techniques. To make the pillow more playful, I made the flower centers from pom poms constructed from yarn in my stash.

NOTE: See "How to Felt and Dye Wool," page 152. There are a number of pom pom makers on the market, and my preference is for the Susan Bates model, which has four mold sizes and results in very nice, even pom poms. Pom poms can also be made using a cardboard circle, although I prefer those from a mold.

1. Iron the wool fabric and cut a square 21 x 21 inches.

2. Cut out the templates as follows:
   - 7 of template A (petals) in rust
   - 7 of template B (petals) in yellow
   - 10 of template C (petals) in orange
   - 3 of template D (small leaves)
   - 3 of template E (medium leaves)
   - 2 of template F (large leaves)

3. For the pillow front, using the photo as a guide, pin the petals to the wool fabric. Leave a space in the center of the petals for the pom poms. With the chenille needle and crewel wool, use the blanket stitch (see page 121) to sew each petal to the front pillow base.

{Continued}

SUPPLIES

- ¾ yard of wool fabric in light blue
- ¾ yard cotton fabric in yellow
- Templates A–F (see "Templates" section, page 197)
- Pins
- Felt fabric scraps in rust, yellow, orange, and green (see note)
- Crewel wool in yellow, red, orange, green, and brown
- Chenille needle
- Worsted-weight wool yarn scraps in assorted colors, for the pom poms
- Susan Bates pom pom maker, with mold sizes 1¼ and 2¼ inches (see note)
- Tapestry needle with large eye
- Fabric glue
- Sewing machine and thread
- Sewing scissors
- 20-inch down pillow form

4. Sew up the center of each leaf with a backstitch (see page 121) to create a vein. Using a simple straight stitch, sew side veins on the leaves. Pin the leaves close to the flowers (see photo). Attach the leaves, using the running stitch (see page 121).

5. Make pom poms using the Susan Bates pom pom maker. Follow the manufacturer's directions. For instructions on how to make multicolor pom poms see page 69.

   FOR THE RUST-COLORED 7-PETAL FLOWER, make 1 multicolor pom pom using the 2¼-inch pom pom maker mold.

   FOR THE YELLOW 7-PETAL FLOWER, make 1 tweeded multicolor pom pom using the 2¼-inch mold. Make 7 solid-color pom poms using the 1¼-inch mold.

   FOR THE ORANGE 10-PETAL FLOWER, make 1 multicolor pom pom using the 2¼-inch mold. Make 8 tweeded multicolor pom poms using the 1¼-inch mold.

6. Attach 1 pom pom to the center of each flower. Using the tail ends of the pom pom and a tapestry needle, stitch the ends through to the pillow back and tie to secure. For the yellow and orange flowers, attach smaller pom poms around the larger pom pom center. Using fabric glue, glue the backs of the pom poms to the center space created when sewing on the petals. Weigh down the whole thing with a book so that the pom poms adhere to the pillow fabric, until the glue is dry.

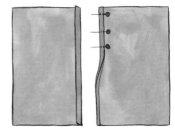

Step 7

7. Make the back of the pillow. Cut the cotton fabric into 2 pieces 21 by 12½ inches. For each piece, fold one 21-inch edge over ¼ inch to the wrong side and press. Fold the edge under again ½ inch and press. Machine-stitch along the fold ⅜ inch from the edge. (See illustration.) If your pillow back fabric has a one-way design, make sure the design is going in the same direction on both pieces before sewing the center edges.

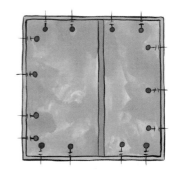

Step 8

8. Lay the decorated pillow front right side up on a table. Place one of the pillow back pieces on top of the embroidery with its right side facing the stitched pillow face, the outer raw edges matching, and the hemmed edge in the center. Pin. Place the other piece right side down, facing the embroidery, with the outer raw edges matching and the hemmed edge in the center. The pieces will overlap in the middle. Pin. (See illustration.)

9. Sew around all 4 sides of the pillow ½ inch from the edge. For neat corners, clip all 4 corners diagonally to remove excess fabric. (See illustration.) Turn

Step 9

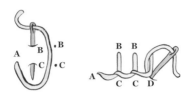

Blanket stitch

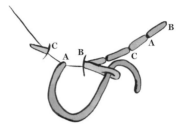

Backstitch

Running stitch

the pillowcase right side out. Using a knitting needle or a capped pen, push out the corners of the pillow from the inside. Press to flatten the seams. Insert pillow form.

BLANKET STITCH: 1. Come up at A. Insert your needle at B and come up at C, but do not pull the needle through until you wrap the thread under the needle. Then, pull the needle through to form a loop that resembles the letter "J." 2. Continue working left to right to form a row of stitches. When your line is complete, go down at D, directly outside the loop, to anchor the stitch.

BACKSTITCH: Come up at A, about ¼ inch from the end of the line. Insert your needle at B, about ¼ inch behind A, and come up at C, ¼ inch beyond A. Pull the stitch through. Continue in this fashion until your line is complete. To finish, stop stitching when you pull your needle through at B.

RUNNING STITCH: Come up at A, and insert your needle at B. Come up at C, and pull the needle through. Continue along the line, keeping the stitches evenly spaced. Once you feel comfortable, you can take several stitches at once.

PAINTED SUNFLOWER
LAMPSHADE

SUPPLIES

- Sunflower layout (see "Templates" section, page 198)
- White fabric lampshade, preferably with Styrene backing
- Dropcloth
- Jacquard Textile Colors in Russet, Goldenrod, Emerald Green, Yellow, Orange, Sapphire Blue, and Brown
- Jacquard #100 Colorless Extender
- Versatex "No Heat" Fixative (eliminates need for heat setting)
- Small deli or yogurt containers for mixing colors
- Auto-fade or vanishing fabric marker
- Artist's paintbrushes in assorted sizes
- Liner brush size 10/0
- Water
- Muslin fabric scraps, for practicing painting

THROUGHOUT OUR HOME I HAVE SEVERAL COLORFUL LAMP-shades that I made by painting white purchased fabric shades. Sometimes I vary the motifs as I paint around the shade. Sometimes I use the same motif, varying the size as I work around. You can copy my motifs or copy motifs from the fabrics in the room where you will be using your lampshade. The design provided here is a simple-to-paint sunflower floral motif. When the lights are on, the shades look like stained glass and they add a warm and pleasant glow to a room. To make a translucent shade, use just one layer of color. Multiple layers may end up looking dark and muddy.

1. Using the sunflower diagram as your guide, practice drawing the sunflower motif a couple of times on paper. Alternatively, if you plan to use a different design, decide upon the motif you want to use. It can be as simple as polka dots or stripes.

2. Spread the dropcloth on your working surface. Thin your textile colors with the Colorless Extender in the lidded containers if you want to lighten the paint colors. Use of the Colorless Extender retains the stained-glass effect of the colors (use of white to lighten the colors will render the lampshade more opaque). Add the Versatex, following the manufacturer's directions.

3. Using the sunflower shade diagram, or your own sketched design, as a guide, practice painting the design on small scraps of muslin or the edge of the dropcloth.

4. Begin painting your lampshade. Use an auto-fade marker or very faint pencil marks to lay out the design. I began by setting up the four sunflowers spaced equally around the shade. Paint the outside rim of each flower center with different colors. Place the outside rims so that the sunflowers will be at different heights on the shade.

{Continued}

5. Next, add the petals, using different colors around each circle. Some of the sunflower petals will not fit on the shade and some will appear to be under the other flowers. Do not overlap the colors.

6. Next, add one or two leaves to each sunflower. There will not be room for complete leaves—some will run off the edge of the lampshade and others will be under the flowers. Let the paint dry completely.

7. Fill in the centers of the sunflowers with polka dots, diagonal stripes, more circles, or whatever you desire with one or more colors.

8. Fill in the background with Sapphire Blue.

9. Outlining the shapes is the fiddliest part of the project, so practice painting around each section of the flowers on a scrap of fabric, using a liner brush and Brown paint. Then paint the outlines on the flowers. Paint veins in the leaves. This will make the design pop.

10. Using Brown, paint the top and bottom rims of the lampshade.

QUIRKY LAMP BASES

For the bases of many of my lamps, I often repurpose pieces of lamps that I find at tag sales and flea markets. These parts don't look like much—just random bits of metal—but these metal pieces can be strung onto a metal-threaded rod and then topped with a lightbulb fixture and a harp to hold a shade. An electrician can do this for you. A spray paint especially formulated for metal can be used to paint the bases.

Pretty old bottles can also be used as lamp bases (see page 167). These are easy to turn into lamps, using a basic kit that you can get at any hardware store. The kit includes a cork that you insert in the bottle opening to hold the lamp harp and electrical parts. To make the bottles more stable, I fill them partway with water. You can also fill bottles with sand, shells, coins, marbles, rocks, and other little collections.

CLOISONNÉ COLLECTION AND BUILDING A COLLECTION OVER TIME

When I go to a flea market or antiques sale, colorful objects and textiles are what I am attracted to. Over a decade ago, I stumbled upon a Japanese cloisonné vase at the Brimfield Antiques Show, which is more like a huge flea market. This first cloisonné vase spoke to me from far across the grassy aisle. The Oriental motifs of flowers, leaves, and birds were familiar. What was so exciting was that the little motifs were edged in metal that created a shiny, colorful object like a piece of jewelry. The price was right, too, because there was some damage to the vase.

Once I got the vase home, I looked into the cloisonné technique a little more and discovered that both China and Japan were known for their highly skilled cloisonné artists. Cloisonné is made by soldering fine wire onto a metal base such as a vase or a bowl. Fine enamel paste is added into the sections between the wires. The objects are fired in a kiln so that the enamel melts onto the base. The result is smooth areas of color separated by thin lines of metal.

As the years pass, I continue to keep my eyes open for cloisonné pieces and pick them up as finances allow. As a group they make a colorful statement when massed on a table—with flowers or without. In the winter, when all the flowers are gone, the vases add jewel-like color to the space.

CH. 6

THE

DINING ROOM

SHORTLY AFTER WE BOUGHT OUR FARMHOUSE, I TRAVELED to England with my friend Sally. We were there for just five short days, but the trip was jammed with nonstop visual intoxication. We toured London at breakneck speed, visiting Leighton House, the Victoria and Albert Museum, Liberty of London and Harrods, the Sir John Soane's Museum, the Bermondsey Flea Market, and more. We rented a car and headed down to Sussex, where we toured Charleston, the famous hand-painted country home of the Bloomsbury artists Vanessa Bell and Duncan Grant, and Monk's House, the home of Virginia Woolf (who was Vanessa Bell's sister). We visited antiques stores where I found some old pottery jugs and great lighting that I used in my kitchen.

The best part of our trip was that I came home inspired to create my own little Charleston in the New England countryside. Trips can do that to me. I soak up as much as I can of the local culture and history of the area I am visiting and add it to my visual memory bank. Later, the ideas will blend together and turn into my own version of decoration.

My husband began buying me antique candle-sticks as Christmas gifts when we were first married. He is just as interested in old things as I am, and it has been nice to grow our collection of antiques together over the years. Eating by can-dlelight gives such a nice atmosphere to any meal. Candlelight can even make grilled cheese sand-wiches taste divine.

When I was a little girl, my mother papered our dining room with an eccentric screen-printed wallpaper full of traveling vines, wacky flowers, squirrels, birds, and monkeys. My sisters and I were horrified and thought she had gone mad. What was wrong with the forest-green walls and ecru trim? We grew to love the paper, and it started many conversations when new friends came for dinner.

My great aunt Jennie's 1920s oak dining set and three sideboards needed a home shortly after we purchased our farmhouse. No one else in the family wanted them. The wood furniture was chunky and intricately carved, and I have fond memories of eating Sunday dinner around the massive table with the inconveniently placed legs. The only problem was that the set was a shade of brown oak I didn't care for. I painted it with a wash of black oil paint and immediately the carving and relief looked rich and voluptuous. I covered the chair seats with a bit of metallic laced sari fabric. I never let a piece of furniture go by if it has good lines and is well built. It can always be made to fit into our home with a bit of paint and elbow grease.

When it came time for me to decorate the walls of our dining room, I pulled together two memories—of the wacky wallpaper from my childhood and of the artistic spirit and no-holds-barred attitude of the Bloomsbury artists at Charleston. Armed with my buckets of latex paint and tubes of artists' acrylics, with design motifs swimming in my head, I dreamed up a mural for our dining-room walls. I painted for four days in between the day-to-day life with my family. As I was painting, I dreamed of the dinner parties we would throw, the conversations that would ensue, the laughter we would share on holidays and birthdays.

I consider myself a proud member of the British decorator Ben Pentreath's "Dining Room Preservation Society"—dedicated to keeping the formal dining room in the design of modern homes. Although we don't use our dining room every day, each Thanksgiving my extended family gathers at our farmhouse for an old-fashioned day in the country. We take a hayride through the hills, stack wood, and come inside to a warm house with a fire blazing to eat turkey with all the trimmings. On the walls the birds and flowers look down on us; they radiate creative inspiration for the lively conversation that is to follow. A dining room holds a special place in family life. Luscious food, candlelight, and conversation become etched in young people's brains, creating irreplaceable memories. Dining rooms are important for cementing relationships over food and drink. When not in use for feasting, a dining room with its big flat table surface can become a cutting table for sewing, a tax preparation table, a wrapping and shipping room, or the place to set things down that need to be out of the fray. It doesn't hurt if the walls are covered with pattern, too.

HOW TO PAINT A MURAL

THROUGHOUT DESIGN HISTORY, PEOPLE HAVE BEEN PAINT-ing murals. The oldest mural known—31,000 years old—was found in a cave in France. Throughout Europe, India, Egypt, Africa, and the world, you can find murals of all kinds done by trained mural painters and untrained homeowners. In the early days of American life, itinerant mural painters traveled the countryside painting walls in what has now become known as the American folk art tradition.

Painting a mural in your own home will add a distinctive artistic flavor to your house. It is not hard to do—the most difficult part is getting up the nerve to do it. Once you decide to give it a go, start researching murals of the past. Combine those with your own ideas and motifs. A mural can have a modern clean-lined aesthetic (perhaps geometric), folk art qualities, or fine brush details. It is up to you to decide what artistic character you want to add to the mural in your home.

Painting a mural like the one in my dining room is not for the timid. The most important thing to remember is that it is only paint and you can make your work disappear quickly simply by painting over it. To get ideas for your own mural, look at wallpaper and fabric designs and murals done in historic homes. Sketch your ideas into a sketchbook to build your confidence and your drawing skills. Decide on a base color to use for the mural. The color you paint your walls will be the dominant color in the room. I chose a dark orange, but you may want a lighter shade, such as robin's egg blue or a sunny yellow. I use a semi-gloss finish because it's more durable than matte finishes.

If you haven't had a lot of experience painting, you might want to practice on hardboard. If you don't feel confident drawing the motifs freehand, cut them out of thin cardboard and trace them onto the walls with pencil. Then fill in the shapes with colors. As you work, you will see your skills improving. Keep going.

SUPPLIES

- Pencil and eraser
- Sketchpad
- Artists' acrylics and latex paint in a selection of colors
- Artist's round and flat brushes
- Artist's liner brushes, sizes 0 and 10/0
- Deli containers with lids for mixing paint
- Water for cleanup

If you don't feel like painting an entire room, creating a mural on one wall or a small corner can be just as effective. I can guarantee you that no one else will have this artwork in their home! Murals are a fabulous way to create a colorful, creative space for your family to enjoy for years to come.

1. Prep your walls by painting a base color.

2. In the sketchbook, draw the different elements you want to include on your wall. I used a selection of leaves and flowers, birds, guinea hens, and bugs. If you are a planner, use graph paper to plan out all your motifs and then scale your designs up to fill your wall.

3. Mix the colors you plan to use. Latex paints and acrylic artist's paints can be intermixed. Use lidded deli containers so that you can keep your mixed paint colors over a few days.

4. With a pencil, draw the curved vertical lines for vines on the walls. Paint them brown or a color of your choosing.

5. Using various colors, add the leaves and vines. Add the birds, then the flowers, then more leaves.

6. When you feel the motifs are working together and the spacing looks good, use a dark color (I used black) and a tiny liner brush (size 10/0) and outline all the designs.

7. Consider placing two different murals next to each other. Below the chair rail at the base of my mural, I worked out a plaid design using blue painter's tape similar to the method I used for the plaid tray (see page 140).

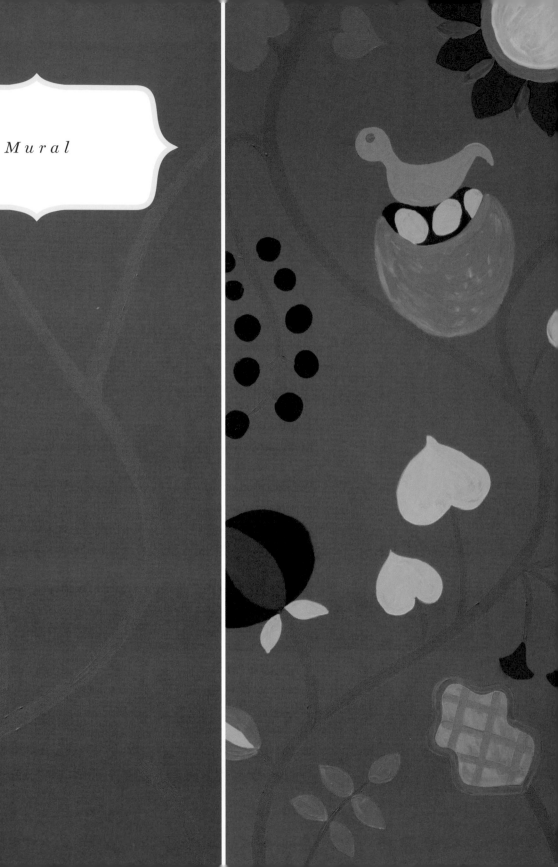

Mural

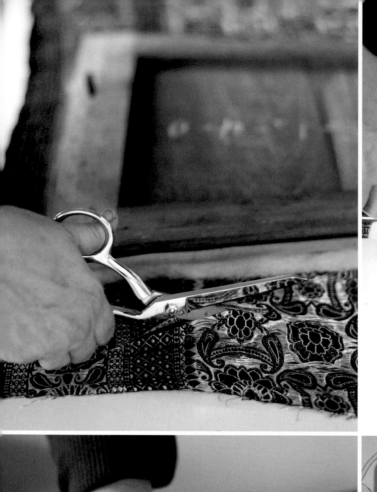

HOW TO RE-COVER A CHAIR SEAT

SUPPLIES

- Fabric for the seat: seat measurement plus 6 inches for each dimension

- Staple gun and ½-inch staples

- Flat-head and Phillips-head screwdrivers

- Quilt batting (optional; this will depend on what you find below the fabric you are removing)

THE SEAT OF A CHAIR IS A GREAT PLACE TO MAKE A COLOR statement. You can use up remnants or flea market finds, as I did with this sari fabric, which I found at an antiques store. Although it can look daunting and mysterious, this is a quick, easy way to spruce up a tired chair.

1. Turn the chair upside down. Unscrew the seat using a screwdriver. Set the screws aside in a safe place to reuse.

2. Remove the staples from the back side of the seat. Remove the fabric.

3. Inside, you will find a piece of wood with stuffing materials. Often you can re-cover the seat without replacing the batting and stuffing. If it is horsehair (a dark brown, stiff fiber), make sure you leave it because it is a valuable component of many old upholstery projects. It can still be purchased but is very expensive.

4. If you have to replace the batting, cut a piece of quilt batting slightly smaller than the wood base. The quilt batting does not wrap around the wood—it should lie on top of the wood base. There is no need to glue it or staple it. If you are replacing worn batting, use the old batting as a cutting guide.

5. Lay your fabric right side down on a table. Center the top of the chair seat with its batting in the center of the fabric. Using scissors, cut around the seat, leaving a 3-inch border all the way around. If you are using a plaid or stripe design, make sure that the fabric is lined up properly so that the lines will be square and even when stapled to the seat.

6. Beginning at one straight side, pull the new fabric to the back and use the staple gun to attach it to the seat. Leave the corners unstapled.

7. On the opposite straight side pull the fabric taut and staple this side. Again, leave the corners free. Repeat for the two remaining angled sides.

8. For the corners, be careful to avoid thick folds on the right side of the seat. Pull the fabric taut, making small pleats at each corner, and staple.

9. Place the chair seat on the chair and, using the original screws, fasten it in place.

PICTURE-FRAME TRAY

I'm always on the lookout for old wooden frames at yard sales and flea markets. Old frames are sometimes chipped and worn but they still have life in them—either for framing photos and paintings or for turning into a handy serving tray. I found this tray at a church sale and paid fifty cents for it—truly one of the best bargains I have ever gotten. It is solid wood and has hand-carved details. The instructions that follow are for the tray that is shown in the photos; of course you can vary things and try out your own color combinations if you prefer.

NOTE: My wooden frame was 25 x 19 inches. Many home stores will cut a piece of plywood for you. Bring your frame with you and explain the project to the staff.

1. Sand the edges of the plywood.
2. Use the flat-head screwdriver to remove any old hanging hardware and staples from the back of the frame. Clean and wash your frame. Let dry.
3. Line up the plywood on the back of the frame where it will be attached. Using a drill, make a pilot hole (smaller than the size of your screw) that goes through the plywood and into the frame. A pilot hole serves as the guide for the wood screw so that it is easier to screw in. Using a drill bit that is slightly larger than the diameter of the screw head, drill a countersink just deep enough so that the screw head is flush with the back surface (so the tray lies flat and doesn't scratch the tabletop). Attach the plywood to the frame with wood screws.
4. Using a foam brush, paint a coat of primer on the tray. Paint the front, back, and sides, letting the primer dry before doing the opposite side.
5. Paint the entire tray with two coats of aqua.
6. Paint the beveled border of the frame green, and paint the little trim section brown.

SUPPLIES

- Wooden picture frame (see note)
- Piece of ½-inch plywood cut to fit the back of the frame (see note)
- 150 grit sandpaper
- Drill with assorted drill bits
- Flat-head screwdriver
- Wood screws and screwdriver
- 1-inch foam brush
- Primer
- Latex paint in aqua, green, brown, red, and topaz
- Painter's blue masking tape
- Ruler
- ½-inch paintbrushes
- Artist's liner brush, size 0
- Walnut-colored stain
- Rag
- Spray polyurethane or spar varnish
- Small round felt furniture protective circles with adhesive

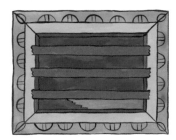

Step 7

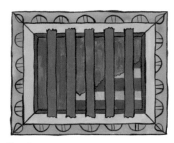

Step 8

7. Paint the plaid detail on the inside tray. To do so, place 3 pieces of 2-inch painter's blue masking tape equally spaced across the horizontal direction of the plywood tray section. Make sure you firmly push the edges of the tape down so that the paint doesn't seep under the tape. Paint the exposed areas red. Let dry and remove the tape. You will have four red stripes. (See illustration.)

8. Place 5 pieces of 2-inch painter's tape evenly spaced vertically across the plywood section. Once again, press down the tape to avoid seeping of paint. Paint the vertical stripes in topaz. Let dry and remove the tape. (See illustration.)

9. With dark brown, paint free-hand stripes using an artist's liner brush on each edge of the stripes to create a plaid-like pattern.

10. Using walnut stain and a rag, wipe stain on the detail areas of the frame, then quickly wipe some of it off leaving it mostly in the recessed areas.

11. To finish, coat with two layers of spray polyurethane or spar varnish. If you expect to be using the tray frequently for liquids, spar varnish will protect the tray from water more effectively.

12. Peel the backing off the felt furniture protectors. Place one on top of each screw on the back of the frame.

POLKA DOT GLASSES

SUPPLIES

- Drinking glasses
- Rubbing alcohol and paper towels
- Dropcloth
- Martha Stewart glass paint in various colors
- Plate or container, for paint
- Foam daubers in various sizes

MOST LARGE CRAFT STORES NOW CARRY PAINT ESPECIALLY made for decorating glass. I chose to do a simple multicolor polka dot design using foam daubers that come in different sizes. This is a simple project that will only take about an hour. The makers of the paint claim it is dishwasher safe, but I prefer to hand wash my glasses to protect the hand-painted designs.

1. Wash the glasses.
2. Wipe the surface of the glasses with a paper towel soaked in rubbing alcohol. This helps the paint to adhere.
3. Lay a dropcloth on your worktable.
4. Squeeze a small amount of paint onto a plate. Dip the foam dauber into the paint and make a dot on the glass. Repeat with different colors. I made 2 patterns: rows of dots in one color and randomly sprinkled dots of many colors.
5. Follow the manufacturer's instructions for curing the paint.

CH. 7

THE

LIBRARY

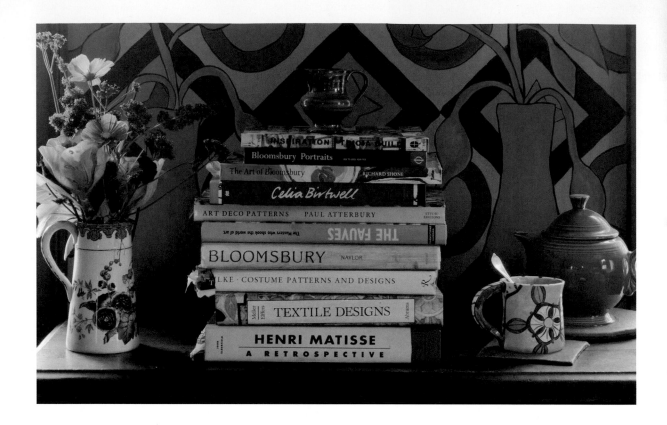

A FEELING OF WELL-USED WARMTH EMBRACES YOU AS YOU enter the library. Immediately, you feel the comfort of loved furniture covered in floral jacquards and oversized checks. The wall of books, full of pattern created by the colorful spines leaning this way and that, creates a feeling that inquisitive, passionate people spend a lot of time in the room. The colors and patterns on the walls, on the floors, on the pillows and lampshades, all blend together to create a curious chaos. It's a room that envelops and is hard to leave.

When I was planning the decoration for the library, I knew that I wanted my collection of textile and craft books to be the main focus of the room. I had Kevin, our contractor, build one large set of shelves to cover an entire wall. Quickly the bookcases, painted in dark charcoal gray, were filled to overflowing with my textile, art, and other books and colorful knickknacks. There is something comforting about a room full of books, about the idea of having the time to read them all, even if it will never actually happen. Books are beautiful objects full of wonderful stories and information. Lots of books packed together in a bookcase or in a stack on the floor or a table create a visual texture that is very appealing.

The library is square and just big enough for a couch, a couple of chairs, and Julia's writing desk. On the walls I wanted to create a feeling of symmetry similar to that of the stone tile floors I saw in Venice. I referred to the colorful illustrations in Owen Jones's *Grammar of Ornament* and set about building a motif I could easily transfer to our walls with paint.

I began by painting the walls a lovely mossy green. I cut out patterns of cardboard FedEx boxes to trace around. Beginning at a corner, I worked my way around the room, dropping plumb lines, tracing around the cardboard models with a pencil. I began with the red cross motif and painted freehand inside my pencil outlines. Green and red are complementary colors, and I was confident I would get the kind of warm feeling I was looking for with these two colors. Next, I added the background square with its triangle extensions centered on the join of the red cross motifs—painting each one a goldish orange. The third element was a simple circle traced into the center of the last layer. I alternated between butter yellow and turquoise to add a little more interest. Last, I added an orange cross motif tipped on its side with an open middle, which let the circle color show through. When all the motifs were painted, I outlined each motif with black, using a liner brush. On a small section of wall between the south-facing windows I painted a simple mural. Two turquoise vases hold stylized flowers. Behind them, I painted a diamond panel similar to the pattern of an argyle sweater.

This room is the coziest in the house. Part of the warmth is from heat from the woodstove and the aged pine boards and mantel. The rest of the warmth is from the colors—the moss green, red, golds, and oranges that I chose to paint the walls and cover the furniture with. If you live in a cold climate, use warm tones to create a warm feeling in your home. If you live in a hot climate, choose cooling shades such as turquoise, blues, greens, and purples. A lot of atmosphere can be created just by the colors you choose.

The furniture is well worn but suits us. I'm rather attached to the fabrics I used when I had the junk-store furniture upholstered many years ago. Taking a cue from the British, I've patched the arms of my favorite knitting chair with a coordinating fabric to cover the holes that have been worn in the arms. Extending the life of any object instead of replacing with new makes sense. This theory may not fit in with modern thinking, but it is right for my family and home. A slightly shabby, improvised look is cozy.

In any room that will be used frequently in the evening, it's nice to include an afghan or throw. Ours are made of wool, but if you live in a warmer climate,

choose cotton. The handmade pillows bring a soft feeling to the room—especially the knit ones, which remind me of cardigans I wear on a cold fall day. Lamps and good lighting are also important for winter rooms, especially if there will be lots of reading and stitching being done. Collections of objects, like the colorful flea market pottery and sheep I display on the mantel, give a room character and detail. I stretched cross-stitch fringed trim from Uzbekistan across the mantel. The resulting room is full of texture and color and warmth.

When creating any cozy space that your family will use, think carefully about

how your family lives, works, eats, and spends time together. Think about the time of year you will be using the room most. Build a space that everyone can feel comfortable in so that you can hang out together. This lovely, cluttered room is a special space to spend an afternoon or to have a quick dinner together in front of the stove in the depth of winter. We "lamb" in midwinter, so frequently there will be a chilled lamb in front of the woodstove getting warm. There is always a black-and-white Border Collie or two or three at our feet and a cat or two looking for space on the couch. We all—pets included—feel safe and happy in this room.

HOW TO FELT AND DYE WOOL

FINDING INTERESTING TEXTILES TO USE TO DECORATE MY home has become a lifelong quest. For years I have worked with items from the thrift shop and repurposed wool and other animal-fiber fabrics to create handmade pillows, bags, and home textile items. When I visit our local thrift store, I am always on the prowl for old wool coats, sweaters, and blankets. Although I like to find light-colored or white textiles, I never pass up a good woolen fabric.

Many of the woolen fabrics I buy I turn into felt. Basically, felt consists of matted, compressed animal fibers. Normally we try to avoid letting our woolens shrink, but the process of felting uses this characteristic of animal fibers. To make homemade felt, simply wash wool or animal fiber fabric in a washing machine with hot water and rinse it with cold water. The change in temperature and the friction in the machine will cause the wool fabric to shrink and become thicker. Felt's advantage for many uses is that it is very dense, and it does not unravel when cut.

Purchased wool felt can be quite pricey, but making your own out of old clothing is extremely economical. Make sure the item is at least 80 percent animal fiber—wool, mohair, alpaca, cashmere, or angora. All of these animal fibers "felt" well—that is, they shrink to make a much denser fabric. (Silk is also a protein fiber, but it does not felt because it doesn't mat and shrink.) If the garment lacks a fiber content label, test the fiber content by doing a burn test on a small piece of the fiber (see "How to Do a Burn Test to Determine Animal Fiber Content," which follows). Fabrics labeled "super-washed" cannot be felted. They are made by chemically treating the fibers so that they do not *shrink.*

{Continued}

HOW TO DO A BURN TEST TO DETERMINE ANIMAL FIBER CONTENT

Cut a 2-inch piece of the fabric near a seam or edge. Unravel or unknit a few of the threads. Light a candle and place it in a sink. Using tweezers, hold the bits of thread in the flame. Observe how they burn. Blow out the flame and look at the residue. Feltable animal fiber smells like a burned human hair, and its residue will be a small, crunchy ball that breaks apart when squished. (Even though silk is not feltable, its fibers will also react the same way to flames. The unburned fiber is usually shiny and not fuzzy.)

HOW TO FELT

Felting is easy if you have the use of a washing machine.

1. Place the fabric, blanket, or garment into a washing machine with your normal laundry detergent. Set the machine for a hot wash and a cold rinse. If you do not have a full load, add some old jeans or sheets to help agitate the fabrics. Do not add bath towels, as they tend to shed fibers that will become imbedded in your wool felt. When the cycle is finished, inspect the fabrics. If the fabrics have not felted enough and the structure of the knit or weave is still visible, run the cycle again.

2. Some wool fabrics need to be felted 3 or 4 times to become thick. Dry the fabric flat.

3. The resulting felt fabric can be cut and used for craft and home decorating projects. It will not unravel when cut.

DYEING WOOL FABRICS AND FELT

Once you have experimented with making your own felt, it is time to begin coloring it. For wool and protein fibers, use dyes commonly called "acid" dyes. They are easy to use, and the results are amazing if you carefully follow the manufacturer's instructions. See "Dyeing Tips," which follows, for getting beautiful colors.

> NOTE: For the enameled pot, a lobster or canning pot works nicely. You'll need it large enough—at least 20 quarts—so that the fabric can float around freely. The pot you use for dyeing cannot be used for any other purpose. A thrift shop is a great place to look for a dye pot. Make sure it is not aluminum.

1. Cut your felt into pieces approximately 18 inches square so they will move around easily in the dye pot. Cut felted garments apart into separate pieces along seams to prevent uneven dyeing, and remove buttons, zippers, and trim.

2. Fill the dye pot two-thirds full of water and begin heating it on the stove.

SUPPLIES

- Felted wool
- Large stainless steel or enamel-coated pot (see note)
- A dust mask, so that you don't breathe in the dye powder
- Rubber gloves
- Disposable mixing containers such as yogurt containers
- ProChemical's PRO WashFast Acid Dye or other acid dyes
- Plastic spoons, for mixing dyes
- White vinegar
- Stove or camp burner

3. Mix the dye. Wearing a mask and gloves and following the manufacturer's directions, measure the powder into a disposable container. Add a small amount of water to form a paste. Add more water to form a thinner liquid. Try to keep it free of lumps—they will result in uneven dyeing. When the dye paste is smooth, stir it into your dye pot of simmering water.

4. Wet the fabric in the sink before placing it in the dye pot. Immersing fabric that is already wet through makes color absorption more even. Follow the dye manufacturer's instructions regarding how much white vinegar to add to the dye bath. Leave your fabric in the dye bath until the water is clear—20 to 30 minutes. The dye is "exhausted" when the water is clear. This means your fabric will not run or bleed.

DYEING TIPS

1. Before immersing the fabric in the dye, wet it completely in the sink or a bucket.
2. The fabric will get lighter as it dries. Keep this in mind when you remove it from the dye pot.
3. All fabrics can be overdyed. If you begin with a light or white fabric, it will be able to be dyed a light shade. You cannot lighten a dark-colored fabric. Darker colors can be overdyed, but it is more difficult to control the outcome. If you dye a color that you aren't happy with, experiment with overdyeing it.
4. Dyeing with chemicals is not kid-friendly. It is best to dye when food is not being prepared. A camp stove for working outdoors is a great alternative to dyeing in the kitchen.
5. Dyeing wool is a fun project to do with a friend. Make a party of it.

PAINTED PILLOW WITH EMBROIDERED SQUIGGLES

SUPPLIES

- ⅝ yard linen fabric in yellow
- Auto-fade or vanishing fabric marker
- Jacquard Textile Paint in Orange
- Flat no. 4 artist's paintbrush
- Crewel wool in turquoise and green (or cotton floss if crewel wool unavailable)
- Embroidery hoop
- ⅝ yard backing fabric in a colorful pattern
- Sewing machine
- 18-inch down pillow insert
- Steam iron

EMBROIDERY IS ONE OF THE EASIEST NEEDLE ARTS TO learn. I began stitching when I was almost a teen, working the crewel kits that were so popular in the 1970s. You don't need any fancy supplies— just some fabric, needle, and thread. It is a portable craft, so unlike with painting and machine sewing, embroidery is a great "on the go" project. For this pillow, I painted the free-form squiggles that became the guides for the added embroidery. Either cotton floss or crewel wool can be used for the embroidery. If you are a beginning stitcher, crewel wool is more forgiving, but it is more difficult to source. Cotton floss is widely available in chain craft stores.

1. Iron the linen base fabric and cut it to measure 17 x 19 inches.

2. Using the auto-fade marker, draw squiggles on the linen fabric, extending them out to the edges of the fabric. These will be your guides for painting.

3. Using fabric paint and a flat brush, paint over the lines. The squiggles should be approximately ⅜-inch wide. Let dry completely. Heat set following the manufacturer's directions.

4. Embroider the pillow. Choose a contrasting color for your backstitch so that it "pops" off the fabric and painted color. I chose bright turquoise and green because they are complementary colors to the yellow fabric and orange paint.

5. Using a backstitch (see illustration, page 121), work around both sides of each squiggle, stitching with one color on each edge.

6. To make the slip-in pillowcase, cut the backing fabric into 2 pieces each 17 x 11½ inches. On each piece, fold under one 17-inch edge ¼ inch to the wrong side and press. Fold the edge under again ½ inch and press. Machine stitch along the fold ⅜ inch from the edge.

7. To assemble the pillow, follow steps 7 and 8 of the instructions to make the Pom Pom Appliqué Pillow (page 120).

EMBROIDERED FELT TRIVET AND COASTERS

WOOL MAKES A GREAT PROTECTOR OF WOOD SURFACES. IT will absorb any liquid that spills and protects a table from heat that could scorch the delicate surface. These felt coasters and trivet are a way to play with complementary colors. Each side is the complementary color of the other side and the chain-stitch embroidery is done with the color from the opposite side. Wool felt is a bit difficult to draw on, so I used a product called tearaway stabilizer to indicate the design on the felt. The design, in this case circles, is traced onto the stabilizer. The stabilizer is pinned to the right side of the felt and the embroidery is worked through both layers. When complete, the stabilizer is ripped away, and the stitched design remains on the felt. I used fabric glue to sandwich the felt together, but hand or machine sewing would also work. The coasters and trivet would make a great gift, tied together with brightly colored yarn.

NOTE: For a bright and fun result, use complementary colors on the front and back of your coasters (see page 6 to learn more about complementary colors). I used teal and orange, yellow and violet, orange and blue, red and green, and yellow-orange and blue-violet. See "How to Felt and Dye Wool," page 152, for directions on how to make felt.

1. Iron the felt using a steam iron.
2. Using the ruler and paper, draw a 5-inch square to make a coaster template.
3. Pin the paper pattern to the felt and cut out 2 squares for each coaster.
4. Cut out a 3½-inch-square piece of tearaway stabilizer. Center a 2½-inch-diameter glass on the stabilizer and trace around it. Pin it to one side of one coaster, with the circle centered on the felt.
5. Using embroidery floss in a color that matches the opposite side of the coaster, work in chain stitch (see illustration) over the center circle, working through the tearaway stabilizer and the felt. Stitch the second coaster piece using an-

SUPPLIES

- Small pieces of wool felt in an assortment of complementary colors (see note)
- Steam iron
- Graph ruler for drawing square
- Paper, for coaster template
- Sulky Tear-EZ tearaway stabilizer
- 2½-inch glass, for tracing circles on tearaway stabilizer
- Embroidery floss in same colors as felt
- 8-inch plate, for trivet pattern
- 4½-inch plate, for tracing circle on trivet
- Fabric glue
- Craft paintbrush

other piece of tearaway stabilizer and the color of the first side. Tear away the stabilizer.

6. Using washable fabric glue and a paintbrush, lightly brush the glue over the wrong side of the one of the coaster pieces. Press the two pieces together, being sure the edges are aligned. The fabric glue will dry a bit stiff and give body to the coaster. Let dry overnight under a heavy book.

7. Cut 2 pieces of felt for the trivet, using an 8-inch plate to make the cutting pattern.

8. On a piece of tearaway stabilizer trace first around the 4½-inch plate, then place the smaller glass in the center of that traced circle and trace around it to make a donut design. Pin the stabilizer on the felt for the trivet with the design centered and embroider the two circles with the complementary color, as for the coasters. Now make a second side, using the same pair of complementary colors. Finish as for coasters.

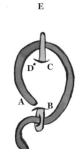

Chain stitch

CHAIN STITCH: 1. Come up at A. Take a stitch from B to C, but do not pull the needle through. Wrap the thread under the needle at C. Pull the needle through and a loop will form on top of the fabric. Continue by inserting your needle at D (inside the loop), then come up at E, again wrapping the thread under the needle before you pull the needle through. 2. To end, insert your needle just outside the loops and pull to the back side to finish the stitch.

STRIPED HAND-KNIT
SCRAP YARN AFGHAN

SUPPLIES

• Color By Kristin yarn by Classic Elite Yarns (50% Wool, 25% Mohair, 25% Alpaca; 93 yards / 50 grams): 2 balls each of the following 22 colors (44 balls total):

Geranium 3258
Lichen 3281
Lady's Mantle 3235
Deep Blue Sea 3248
Aubergine 3226
October Leaves 3278
Raspberry 3232
Yarrow 3243
Julia's Pink 3289
Spring Green 3215
Cornflower 3257
Pumpkin 3285
Turquoise Seas 3246
Lamb's Ears 3249
Deep Forest Green 3212
French Roast 3276
Caramel 3244
Sunflower 3250
Coleus 3260
Blue Thyme 3220
Rock Henna 3255
Anemone 3295

• 1 24-inch-long circular knitting needle size US 8

GAUGE

4 stitches = 1 inch in both garter and reverse stockinette stitch ridges

*LIKE MOST KNITTERS AND CROCHETERS, I HAVE AN IMPRES-*sive stash of leftover balls of yarn. This project is designed to use them up. This striped afghan design is a great project for stash-busting your odds and ends of yarns. It can be made over a series of months, even years. This afghan uses a total of twenty-two different colors; of course the colors can be modified to match your stash of scraps.

Five panels are made out of scraps of colors using a simple reverse stockinette ridge stitch, knitted on a circular needle. I chose this stitch because the knitted material lies flat when completed and the back has an interesting texture and color pattern. The strips are sewn together and the yarn ends are tied so that they become a decorative fringe on the back side. I've used worsted-weight yarns here, but the design can easily be adapted to be larger or smaller by changing the number of stitches or panels or by using a heavier- or lighter-weight yarn (but use the same weight yarn for the whole project). If you use a bulkier yarn, the afghan will turn out larger, heavier, and warmer.

FINISHED SIZE: 48 X 60 INCHES

NOTE: Because this project doesn't need to fit anyone, gauge is not that important. An afghan should drape and be comfortable to snuggle under, so choose your needle size accordingly for a relatively loose fabric.

PATTERN STITCHES

GARTER STITCH

All rows: Knit all sts.

REVERSE STOCKINETTE STITCH RIDGES

Rows 1 and 2: Knit all sts.

Row 3: Purl all sts.

{Continued}

Slip the stitches to the opposite end of the needle following row 3 and then begin another color. This eliminates many purl rows.

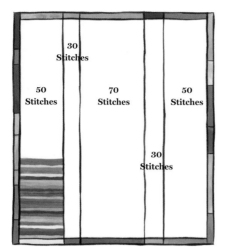

Afghan Chart

You will make 5 pieces: 2 medium (panel 1), 2 narrow (panel 2), and 1 wide (panel 3). The stripe sequence should vary among the panels to make a random patchwork color effect. Make sure that the colors contrast with each other. For example, don't put two blues next to each other unless one is very dark and the other, very light. Place complementary color pairs in stripe sequences following each other.

PANEL 1 (MAKE 2)

Using chosen color and circular needle, CO 50 sts. Knit 7 rows. Break first color, leaving a 6-inch tail.

Join the second color, leaving a 6-inch tail, tying it with a knot with the last color of yarn close to the fabric. Work the next three rows in reverse stockinette stitch ridges.

Break yarn, leaving a 6-inch tail. Slip all sts onto the opposite end of the circular needle.

Continue in this manner repeating the reverse stockinette stitch ridge stitch pattern and changing colors after 3 rows are complete. Remember to slip the just-knit stitches to the opposite end of the needle after each stripe is complete and to tie the tails of the yarn together.

Work until the piece measures 47 inches and you have completed a stripe. Slip stitches to the opposite end of the needle. Join another color and knit 7 rows. BO all sts neatly.

HINT: When the strips get too long and cumbersome, roll them up, beginning at the cast-on edge, and secure with a knitting needle.

PANEL 2 (MAKE 2)

Using the chosen border color, CO 30 sts. Make as for panel 1, but the colors should not repeat—they should be random. Do not begin or end the panels with the same border colors.

PANEL 3 (MAKE 1)

Using chosen border color, CO 70 sts. Make as for panel 1, but the colors should not repeat—they should be random. Do not begin or end the panels with the same border colors.

ASSEMBLE PANELS

Following the chart, sew the stripe panels together using a mattress stitch (see illustration, page 187). Tie all the ends together if not already done. At the ends of the strands that are tied together, tie a second overhand knot. Vary the lengths between the knots so there will be an uneven-looking fringe at the back. Each tied strand will have 2 knots—one close to the fabric and one a few inches away from the knot.

VERTICAL BORDER

The sides are finished with thin blocks of different colors of garter stitch.

With the circular needle, pick up and knit 1 st for every 2 rows along one side, picking up a random number of sts so just a small portion of the side is knit in one color. Work in garter stitch for 7 rows. BO. Pick up and knit a second random number of sts (1 st for every 2 rows) and repeat. Work in garter blocks until the entire vertical edge has a border. Repeat on the other vertical side, changing the color and the number of stitches you pick up and knit each time so that each garter stitch section is a different size. Using the tail ends, sew the small seams where the garter stitch sections join.

BOOKS OF INSPIRATION

There is nothing more enticing to me than to see shelves full of books in a person's home. It is an inside peek into their passions and interests. Building a library is a long process. Buying new books, buying old out-of-print books, and creating a collection is a pleasant hobby. Internet search engines make it much easier than it used to be to find older books that still hold valid content for learning to make things and decorate. Library book sales are favorite stops of my daughter's and mine as we both continue to build our collection of words and photos. Here are some of my favorite books on textiles and decorating.

Complete Book of Painting Techniques for the Home, by Annie Sloan. Annie Sloan has written more than twenty books on painting and color, and they all are great.

Embroidered Textiles: A World Guide to Traditional Patterns, by Sheila Paine. Sheila Paine is a prolific author of great textile books.

English Decoration: Timeless Inspiration for the Contemporary Home, by Ben Pentreath.

Erica Wilson's Embroidery Book, by Erica Wilson.

Fabric Surface Design, by Cheryl Rezendes.

Full-Color Picture Sourcebook of Historic Ornament, by Auguste Racinet.

Glorious Interiors, by Kaffe Fassett. All of his books are inspirational.

Grammar of Ornament, by Owen Jones.

Hand Dyeing Yarn and Fleece, by Gail Callahan.

Inspiration and *Tricia Guild Pattern,* by Tricia Guild. All of Tricia Guild's books are fabulous.

Paint Recipes: A Step-by-Step Guide to Colors and Finishes for the Home, by Liz Wagstaff.

Russian Textiles: Printed Cloth for the Bazaars of Central Asia, by Susan Meller.

Textile Designs: Two Hundred Years of European and American Patterns Organized by Motif, Style, Color, Layout, and Period, by Susan Meller and Joost Elffers.

INSPIRATION TRICIA GUILD

Bloomsbury Portraits RICHARD SHONE

The Art of Bloomsbury RICHARD SHONE

Celia Birtwell ST. MARTIN'S PRESS

BONNARD Sarah Whitfield
John Elderfield ABRAMS

sett Kaffe Fassett's GLORIOUS INTERIORS Little, Brown

ECO PATTERNS PAUL ATTERBURY STUDI
EDITIO

The Masters who shook the world o THE FAUVES PARKSTONE
AURORA

OOMSBURY NAYLOR Bulfinch

E · COSTUME PATTERNS AND DESIGNS

Meller | Elffers TEXTILE DESIGNS Abrams

HENRI MATISSE
A RETROSPECTIVE THE MUSEUM OF MODERN ART
NEW YORK

CH. 8

THE UPSTAIRS BEDROOMS *AND* STAIRWAY

OUR HOUSE ISN'T VERY LARGE OR GRAND. IT IS EASY TO
imagine an early American family living in it, adding to the living space as time
and finances allowed. At the end of the living room, a small open, curved stairway
leads to the two bedrooms above. To visually separate the stairway space from
the living-room space, I decorated it with different colors and gave it its own wall
treatment. Because the stairway is visible at all times, the wall treatment had to
blend with the décor of the living room. I colorwashed the walls to create a pretty
turquoise background, painted stripes, and then stamped the walls to create a faux
wallpaper treatment. I treated the stairs themselves to a colorwash in splotchy
layers of orange and slate blue and covered it with a wash of olive green. As the
painted stairs wear, the different colors show through.

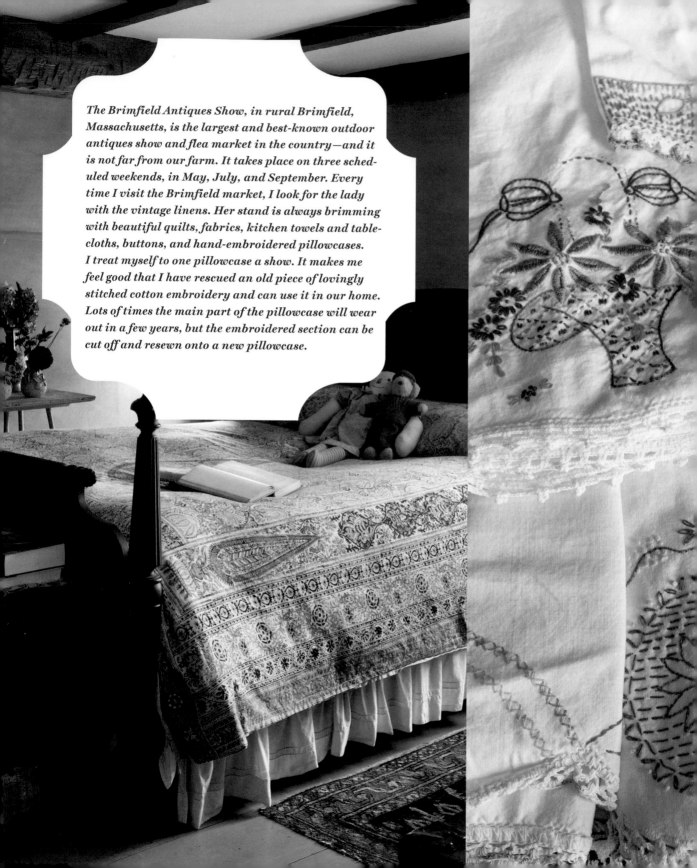

The Brimfield Antiques Show, in rural Brimfield, Massachusetts, is the largest and best-known outdoor antiques show and flea market in the country—and it is not far from our farm. It takes place on three scheduled weekends, in May, July, and September. Every time I visit the Brimfield market, I look for the lady with the vintage linens. Her stand is always brimming with beautiful quilts, fabrics, kitchen towels and tablecloths, buttons, and hand-embroidered pillowcases. I treat myself to one pillowcase a show. It makes me feel good that I have rescued an old piece of lovingly stitched cotton embroidery and can use it in our home. Lots of times the main part of the pillowcase will wear out in a few years, but the embroidered section can be cut off and resewn onto a new pillowcase.

We tend to live mostly on the main floor of our house, only escaping to the bedrooms when it is time to collapse into bed. The rooms are basic and utilitarian and painted in soothing solid colors that add a sense of calm. I've used pattern on the bedspreads and in the rugs. Books are piled along the walls—books to be read and books that have been read. Beside each bed is a solid table or chest of drawers with a lamp for bedtime reading.

Massive dark wood beams and very low ceilings are the prevalent visual feature in the bedroom in the oldest part of the house. I colorwashed the walls a shade of pink, which turned out to be the perfect choice—the room looks bright at night, and the color is subtle during the day. I thought about painting the dark beams white but instead chose to keep the history of the wood structure of the house intact. I am all for living in the modern world, but I also feel that homeowners should respect the past of their homes. Before drastically changing the antique character and period details of any home, think about how you can work with a detail, such as the dark wood in this room, in order to layer the present with the past.

I like to keep bedrooms simple, focusing on the quiet countryside that is outside. In the "new" bedroom, I painted the walls the brownish color of a peach pit. It sets off the wood furniture and is a peaceful color day and night. In the winter, we wake to see the mountain beyond covered with snow. In the spring the enormous ancient maple tree's leaves unfurl in my favorite shade of chartreuse. In the summer the birds sing. In the fall the maple tree is a blaze of orange and gold summoning the fires in the woodstove that are to come.

Bedrooms are about quiet and comfort. Once again, textiles can be the good bones to a good room. Wool and down comforters warm us in the winter. Lightweight cotton spreads make the summer heat bearable. Textiles do the job—adding ambience, balance, and serenity to a sleeping space.

On the east side of the bedroom where the sun comes up each morning, I have a Victorian-era wood desk. I placed it along this wall because just the thought of sitting and writing letters in longhand makes me dream of earlier, slower times. Every night I read in bed before falling asleep. I stack all the read books along the floor as a record of "books I have read." When I awake, it is a pretty and inspirational site—books read, letters and books written—even if I now do most of my writing on a laptop.

I don't think a house can ever have too many paintings. There is always room to hang another—on a wall or even on a closet door. Paintings add color and interest to a room. This is one of the first oil paintings I ever attempted when Julia was an infant. It is of zinnias in a glass vase. It is nice to keep a record of how your art changes as your skills build over the years.

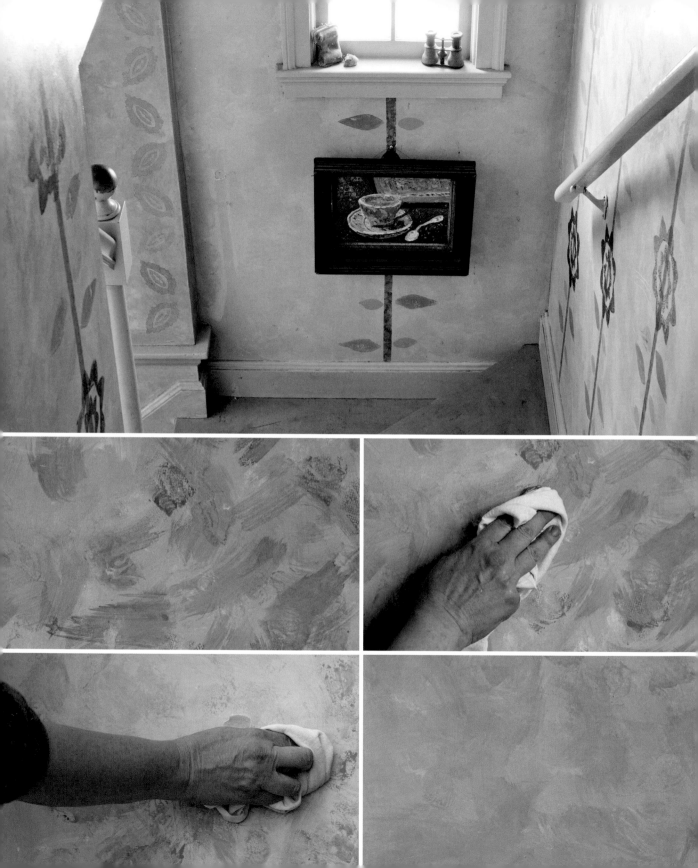

HOW TO COLORWASH A WALL

SUPPLIES

- Latex paint, for the base color (see note)
- Roller
- 1-inch brush, for cutting in at ceiling and floor
- Latex paint in assorted colors, for the base coat and layering (see note)
- Latex paint, for the top colorwash (see note)
- Plastic paint containers (available at paint stores)
- Turkish towel or rags, for wiping on paint
- Texturizing materials such as plastic bags, paper bags, plastic wrap, bubble wrap, or paper
- Polyurethane

COLORWASHING SUPPLIES

Old towels work great for colorwashing walls. Purchase them at thrift stores or ask your friends to save them for you. Lint-free rags, old sheets, and sponges can also be used for colorwashing.

COLORWASHING IS AN EASY DECORATIVE PAINTING TECH-nique that creates mottled, visually textured walls with a soft, pretty look. Colorwashing involves using a rag or towel to splotch one or more shades on top of a light-colored base coat, then applying an overall wash in a top color. It is a great treatment for high-traffic areas because bumps and dings will not be as obvious as they are on solid-colored walls. It is one of those projects that doesn't look too good in the early stages, but once the final color is washed on, it is gorgeous. The final color will dominate the wall's appearance.

NOTE: I used light blue for the base color and layered it with white, blue, umber, and yellow. For the top colorwash I used turquoise.

1. Apply the base coat to the walls with a brush or roller. Let dry.
2. Pour a small amount of one of the middle-layer colors into a large paint container. Thin it with water to the consistency of heavy cream. With a brush, plastic bag, sponge, or a rag, blot on little bits of the color. These marks should be random. Repeat with the remaining colors for layer 2. You should leave some areas of the base color showing through. Vary the spacing and the amount of each color over the wall. It is easier to work one color all the way around the room, then the next. Let dry. These diluted colors will dry rather quickly.
3. Dilute the top-layer color with water to the consistency of heavy cream. You will need quite a bit of this color for the colorwash step. Soak a Turkish towel or rag with the final color. Using large sweeping motions, wash the walls with the paint. Near the trim and ceiling, use a smaller rag and take care to be neat. Let dry. Do a second coat of paint if you want a more opaque look.
4. For high-traffic areas, cover with polyurethane to seal.

HOW TO PAINT STRIPED AND FLORAL "WALLPAPER"

I'VE ALWAYS LOVED THE LOOK OF WALLPAPER, BUT NOT THE price. It is also messy to apply and is a pain to remove. When painting the stairway in our home, I designed an easy decorative paint treatment that looks like a striped wallpaper design. To make the faux wallpaper design, I began by painting mottled one-inch stripes evenly spaced across the wall. I then stamped the floral shape over the stripe to make another pattern layer. Last, I added orange and gold leaves randomly spaced up each side of the stripes. The stamped effect is handmade looking, and it nicely complements the colorwash treatment of the wall.

This project is very quick to do. Making sure the stripes are straight requires some care, but the extra flower and leaf details are randomly placed. You can experiment with many variations such as thick and thin stripes, many different flowers, closer or farther spacing—the list is endless. If you are nervous about trying this, practice on a large piece of cardboard to get over your jitters.

NOTE: I used dark blue and olive green for the stripes and royal blue, gold, and orange for the flowers and leaves.

1. Determine the spacing for the stripes. Stripes may be positioned evenly across your wall or unevenly, at random distances apart.
2. For each stripe, hold the level vertically and use a pencil to lightly draw a straight line up the entire wall. Tape along the pencil line with the blue masking tape, making sure that the pencil line will be covered with paint.
3. Decide how wide you want your stripe. If it will be 3 inches wide, use the ruler to measure this distance from the first piece of tape and make a series of light marks all the way up the wall 3 inches from the first piece of tape. Tape the

{Continued}

SUPPLIES

FOR THE STAMPS

- Templates A–C (see "Templates" section, page 200)
- Kids' fun foam with adhesive backing for making stamps
- 1-inch-thick foam building insulation (often called gray or blue board)
- Scissors
- Tape
- Utility knife

FOR THE "WALLPAPER"

- Long builder's level
- Ruler
- Pencil
- 1-inch-wide painter's blue masking tape
- Latex paint in assorted colors, for stripes, flowers, and leaves (see note)
- Dauber, stippling brush, or other stiff brush
- 1-inch foam brush

painter's tape along the marks. Press the edges of all the tape down firmly with your fingers to make sure you get a good seal, so that the paint can't seep under the edge.

4. With your paint and your stippling brush, dauber, or stiff brush, use a quick pouncing motion to paint between the two pieces of tape. Let dry and remove the tape. To mottle the stripe as I did, dip half the tip of the stippling brush into one color and the other half into a second color. Pounce randomly along the stripe to mix the colors. Repeat until all stripes are complete.

5. Prepare your stamps. Referring to the instructions on "How to Make a Stamp for Printing Fabric and Walls" on page 84, make stamps using templates A–C.

6. Using your stamp from template A (the floral stamp), stamp the flower motif randomly over the stripes, applying the paint with the foam brush. To finish the faux wallpaper, use the stamps from templates B and C (the leaf stamps) to print two colors of leaves on either side of the stripe.

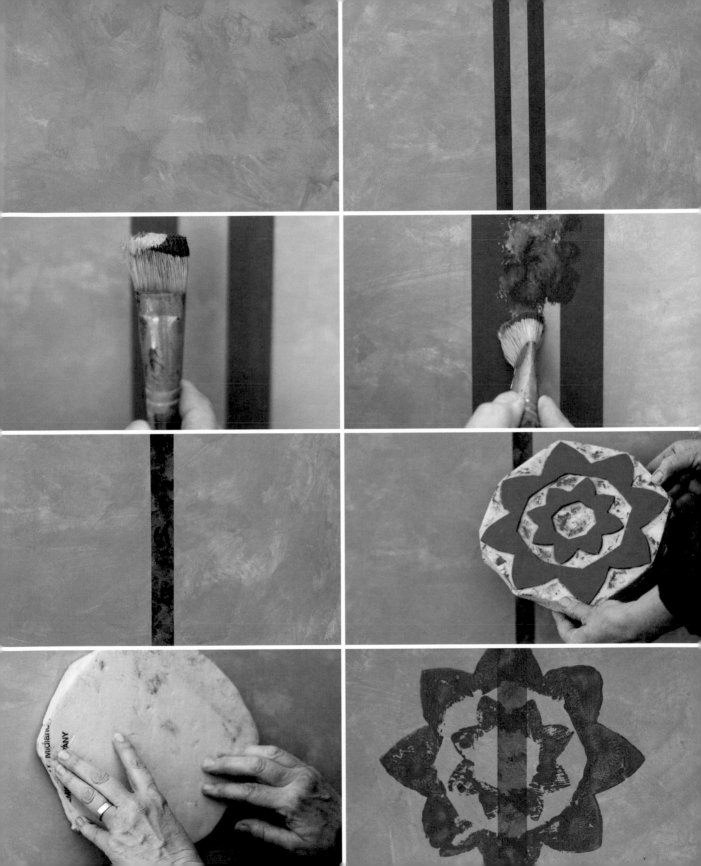

BLOCKS-AND-BRICKS
DUVET COVER

SUPPLIES

- ¾ yard each of 6 colors of 45-inch quilting fabric, for the blocks (see note)

- ¾ yard each of 2 colors of 45-inch quilting fabric, for the bricks

- 2 yards of 45-inch quilting fabric, for the border

- 5 yards of 45-inch-wide quilting fabric, for the back cover

- 5 yards 45-inch-wide muslin, for backing the patchwork (optional)

- Embroidery floss, for tying optional muslin backing

- Steam iron

- Graph ruler

- Sewing machine

- Rotary fabric cutter

- Scissors

- Seam ripper

- One 54-inch zipper or hook-and-loop fastener

I WILL ADMIT THAT I AM NOT MUCH OF A QUILTER. WHILE I love quilts and the artistry that is involved in making them, we prefer down comforters covered in colorful duvet covers and wool blankets on our beds because the old farmhouse is very chilly in the winter. For this project I took the piecework that I love from quilts, made a simple pattern based on squares and rectangles, and colored it with very bright and contrasting solid colors. To give it visual weight, I chose a dark eggplant color for the border. Instead of quilting my piecework, I inset a zipper at the bottom and used it to cover a down duvet.

The blocks-and-bricks design is easy to piece and, because of how I have placed the shapes, there isn't much matching up of seams. You can choose to quilt and bind it traditionally or inset a zipper or a hook-and-loop fastener (such as Velcro) at the bottom edge and use it as a duvet cover as I did. I backed my quilt with a sunflower-themed fabric I designed myself and had printed digitally at Spoonflower.

FINISHED SIZE: 82 X 92 INCHES TO FIT A FULL-SIZE DOWN COMFORTER. TO ADJUST SIZE, INCREASE THE BORDER PIECES IN LENGTH AND WIDTH.

NOTE: Selecting the colors and fabrics for your duvet cover is where the fun starts. For the blocks I used red, green, orange, turquoise, light orange, and fuchsia; for the bricks, purple and lime green; and for the border, dark eggplant. Use the template provided to design your own color version. To do this, photocopy the chart onto cardstock. Cut small pieces of fabric in colors or prints of your own choosing. Attach the colors to the chart with double-sided tape. You can play all you want with them until you have a design you like. Use the chart as your road map when sewing the quilt.

{Continued}

1. Wash to preshrink all fabrics. Iron to neaten before cutting.

2. Using a rotary cutter, cut your fabrics as follows: For the blocks, cut 5 blocks from each color measuring 13 x 13 inches. For the bricks, cut 10 pieces from each color measuring 5 x 13 inches, and 4 pieces measuring 5 x 7 inches. For the border, cut 4 pieces measuring 44 x 9 inches for the top and bottom borders and 4 pieces measuring 39 x 8 inches for the side borders.

3. Sew the blocks together, 6 blocks per strip, in the order shown in the chart. Sew the bricks together in the order shown with half bricks at each end. Use a ½-inch seam allowance when sewing all pieces.

4. Assemble the strips of blocks and bricks as shown on the chart. Sew the strips together.

5. Sew two 44 x 9-inch border strips together on one short side to make the top border. Repeat for bottom border. Sew two 39 x 8-inch strips together on one short side to make one side border. Repeat for the opposite side.

6. Sew the 2 short borders to each side of the quilt. Sew the longer borders to top and bottom of quilt.

7. If you are adding muslin backing to the patchwork, cut 2 pieces 93 inches long. Sew them together along 1 selvage edge. Press the seam open. Lay the muslin backing onto a table seam side up. Lay the patchwork top, seam side down, onto the muslin. Pin in multiple places. Using embroidery floss, tie the muslin to the pieced top at the seams. Backing the pieced section will prevent excess fraying when the cover is laundered.

8. Cut 2 pieces of the back cover fabric 93 inches long. Sew them together along 1 selvage edge. Measure your patchwork top and adjust the width of the back cover fabric to match the width of the top, making sure the seam on the back fabric remains in the center.

9. Place the pieced top and the back fabric with the right sides together, aligning all edges. At the bottom edge, determine the center of the piece and mark. Pin the bottom edge. Center the zipper and mark the 2 end-points of the zipper opening with pins or a marker. (See illustration.) Sew along the bottom edge, beginning at one end in a regular-length stitch, changing to a basting-length stitch when you reach the mark where the zipper will begin, then changing back to a regular-length stitch for the remainder of the seam after you pass the other mark showing the end of the zipper. Press the seam open.

10. Inset the zipper using the centering method: Place the right side of the zipper

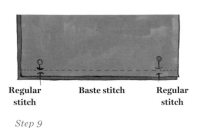

Regular   **Baste stitch**   Regular
stitch   **stitch**

Step 9

Step 10

Backing fabric

Duvet Chart

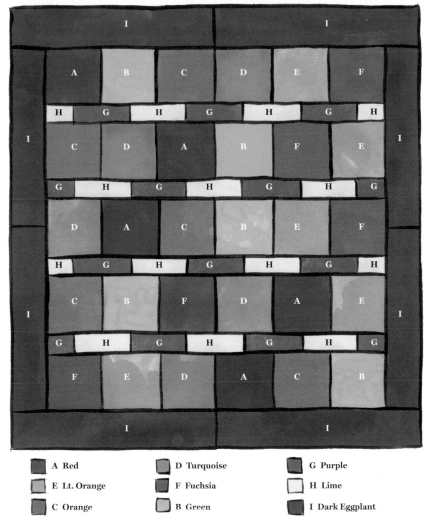

	A Red		D Turquoise		G Purple
	E Lt. Orange		F Fuchsia		H Lime
	C Orange		B Green		I Dark Eggplant

toward the basted seam, centering it. Pin it in place. Using a zipper foot, stitch across the bottom of the zipper, stitch ⅜ inch away from the zipper up one side, stitch across the other end of the zipper, then down the remaining side ⅜ inch away from zipper. After the zipper is sewn in, remove the basting stitches with a seam ripper.

11. With right sides together, and the zipper partly open, pin and sew the remaining 3 sides of the duvet cover to the backing as if you were making a giant pillow. Clip the corners diagonally. Turn the cover right side out. Press and insert your duvet cover.

CRAZY QUILT SWATCH BLANKET

FOR MANY YEARS I HAVE BEEN DESIGNING KNITWEAR PRO-fessionally, writing instructions for knitters to follow. Each design begins with a knitted swatch where I experiment with the yarn, the colors, and cable patterns, and determine the stitch gauge and color charts. If you are familiar with knitting, you know how important the swatching step is to a successful finished project. Never one to toss out something that might be useful someday, I have saved all the swatches for reference, keeping them packed away in mothballs. I am so happy to have found a use for these pretty pieces of textile design.

If you are a knitter or crocheter, you can make this project with your saved swatches. As you stitch the swatches together, you will remember the time in your life when you were making the project that began with each swatch. This is a slow project and can continue for many years. I chose not to back my blanket with fabric, because I may add more swatches to it as I make them, but you could hand sew a pretty quilting fabric to cover the wrong side if you wish.

You may not have as many swatches as I do, or may not be a knitter or crocheter. You can make a blanket similar to this by purchasing old sweaters at thrift stores or cutting up those you already own and perhaps no longer wear. You may have old baby sweaters from your child that you have been saving. This is a perfect project to use the old sweaters and then gift the blanket to your child or keep as a memory.

All of my swatches were different sizes. Assembling the blanket was sim-ilar to doing a giant jigsaw puzzle. I began by hand sewing similarly sized pieces together, using a mattress stitch. Slowly, I kept adding the swatches, one by one, positioning them where the colors looked nice and where they fit. This is a free-form project with no particular planning necessary. It will grow organically.

If the colors of your swatches don't look good together, they can be dyed.

SUPPLIES

- Small knit and crochet swatches or old sweaters (I used wool and animal fiber blends)
- Tapestry needle
- Assorted colors of yarn
- Scissors
- Pins and pincushion
- Sewing machine for resizing swatches and sweater pieces (optional)

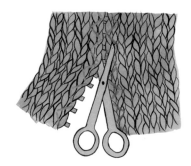

Cutting knit fabric.

Mattress stitch on stockinette stitch.

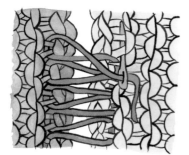

Mattress stitch on bound-off edge to bound-off edge.

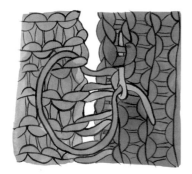

Mattress stitch on garter row to bound-off edge.

I had many white and beige swatches that I dyed to make them better fit the color range of the majority of my swatches (see "How to Felt and Dye Wool," page 152).

1. Wash your swatches or sweaters and lay them flat to dry.

2. To cut swatches from sweaters, use a sewing machine to zigzag-stitch at a medium stitch width and length between 2 rows of stitches or rows about ⅛ inch away from each other, in squares or rectangles of varying shapes. Cut between the 2 rows of zigzag stitching to make swatches that will not unravel (see illustration).

3. Pin together 2 similar-size swatches side by side. Sew together by hand using a mattress stitch (see illustrations). When joining swatches with different gauges, careful pinning can help ease the two pieces together.

4. If you have trouble fitting certain pieces into the design, cut the swatches to fit as described in step 2.

5. Make 1 section at a time. I made 3 sections, with a straight side on either side. To sew the large sections together, I placed them on a large table and pinned them, then sewed them together by hand, using the table for stability.

6. Wash the blanket carefully. It will be quite heavy, so pick a day when it will dry quickly. Spread it out on a large bed or outside and smooth out the fabric. Let dry.

SQUARES-AND-CIRCLES CURTAIN

I LOVE TO SEE WHITE CURTAINS BLOWING IN THE BREEZE on a new spring day. The translucency and weave of the structure of the fabric are irresistible. I have always been able to get lost in such delicate, simple beauty. The Circles-and-Squares Curtain combines a pretty linen curtain with simple geometric shapes added with paint and chain stitch embroidery. You'll want to use translucent fabric paint so that the texture of the fabric shows through.

NOTE: I used a cotton fabric curtain 42 inches wide and 52 inches long.

1. Iron the curtain.

2. Lay the curtain out on a flat surface. Using the ruler and auto-fade marker, draw a straight line parallel to the bottom edge 6 inches up from the bottom of the curtain.

3. Using the graphed ruler, draw a 2-inch square on a piece of cardboard. Cut it out to use as a template.

4. Trace around the rim of the larger glass on a piece of cardboard. Center the smaller glass within the circle and trace around it to form a donut pattern. Cut around the outer circle. Cut the center circle away. The resulting donut shape will be your circle template.

5. Determine the placement of your templates. To start, find the center of the curtain and make a mark along the horizontal line. Measure 4 inches in from either side of the curtain and make a mark along the horizontal line. Center the circle template, then trace the circle motif at each of these three points— one on each side of the curtain and one in the center—using the auto-fade marker. Determine the center point between the circles on each side and trace another circle at each point. You will now have 5 circles. (Depending on the width of your curtain, you can vary the number of repetitions.)

SUPPLIES

- White linen or cotton curtain to fit your window (see note)
- Graph ruler
- Auto-fade or vanishing fabric marker
- Jacquard Textile Color in Pink and Olive Green
- Embroidery floss in pink and olive-green
- Scissors
- 2 glasses, about 2 inches and 4 inches in diameter, to make a "donut" template
- Cardboard
- Dropcloth
- Small artist's paintbrush

6. Using the square template, trace a square halfway between each circle, centering the square on the horizontal line. There will be 4 squares.

7. Using fabric paint, mix the desired colors. Lay the dropcloth on a smooth, wide surface and place the curtain on it. Paint the motifs. Let dry. Heat-set following the fabric paint manufacturer's directions.

8. Embroider the curtain. Embroidery floss is made of 6 thin strands of cotton. I used 3 strands for this project. If you want a heavier look, stitch with more strands. The pink circles are edged in green and the green squares are edged in pink. Work in chain stitch (see page 159) ¼ inch away from each shape. Each circle had two rows of stitching, inside and outside the donut shape.

9. Press and hang.

TEMPLATES

Motif Template

A. Four Petal Flower

B. Three Leaves

C. Giant Paisley

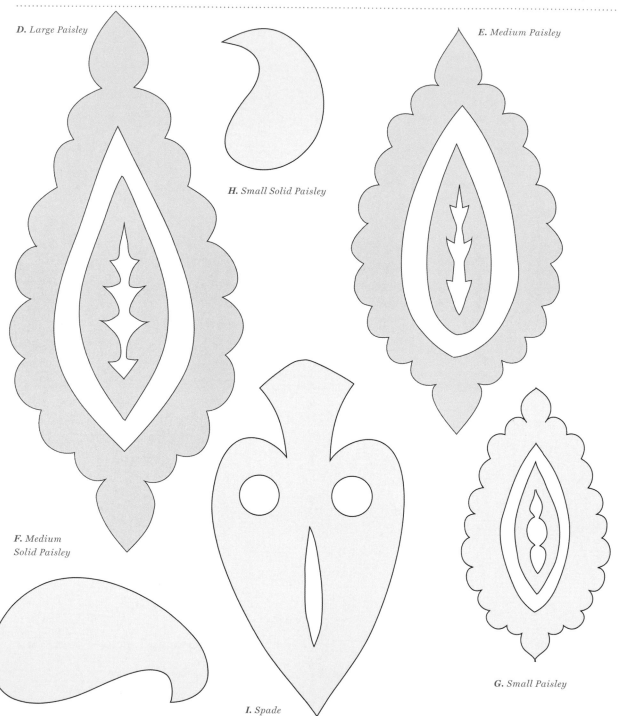

D. *Large Paisley*

E. *Medium Paisley*

H. *Small Solid Paisley*

F. *Medium Solid Paisley*

I. *Spade*

G. *Small Paisley*

SCOTT'S HAND-STAMPED ROCKING CHAIR PAD
(CHAPTER 4)

Increase by 276%

Chair Pad Template

19"

A.

B.

C.

POM POM APPLIQUÉ PILLOW (CHAPTER 5)

Shown at full size

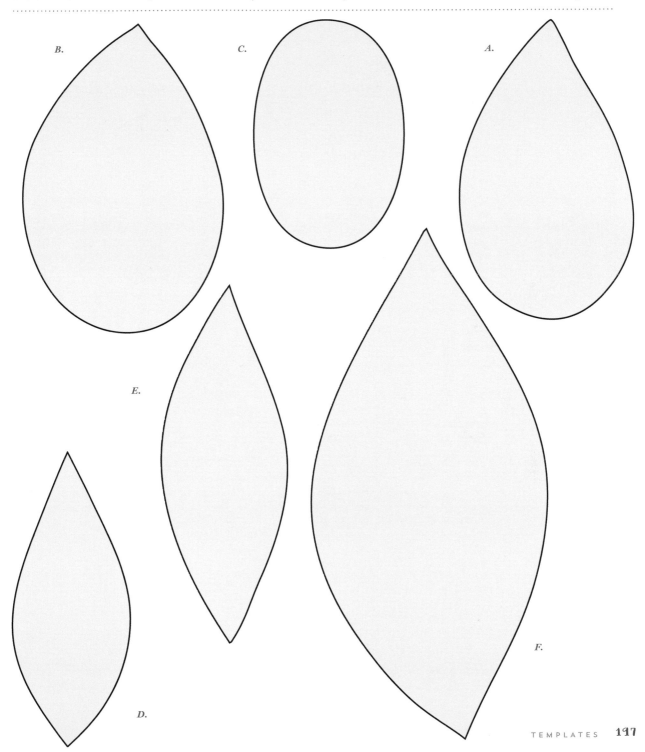

B.

C.

A.

E.

D.

F.

Sunflower Layout

A.

B.

C.

MAGAZINES FOR INSPIRATION

The World of Interiors (www.condenast.co.uk/world-of-interiors). My favorite decorating magazine, with fabulous articles and photos of stunning homes all over the world.

Selvedge Magazine (www.selvedge.org). Published in the UK, with inspirational articles on textiles.

Country Living Magazine (www.allaboutyou.com/countryliving). A nicely styled British country–inspired magazine.

Elle Décor (www.elledecor.com). There are many other versions of *Elle Décor* from countries all over the world.

House Beautiful (www.housebeautiful.com).

VENDORS USED IN KITCHEN RENOVATION

CABINETS: Crown Point Cabinetry, Claremont, New Hampshire (www.crown-point.com).

SINK: Shaw's fireclay farmhouse sink imported to the United States by Rohl (www.rohlhome.com).

FAUCET: Perrin and Rowe faucet imported to the United States by Rohl (www.rohlhome.com).

SCHIST COUNTERTOP: Ashfield Stone, Shelburne Falls, Massachusetts (www.ashfieldstone.com).

KNITTING AND CROCHET YARN

Color by Kristin (Wool/Mohair/Alpaca blend), distributed by Classic Elite Yarns (www.classiceliteyarns.com) and available in local yarn stores.

EMBROIDERY SUPPLIES

COTTON EMBROIDERY THREAD

All major craft and sewing chain stores carry embroidery floss and pearl cotton.

WOOL EMBROIDERY THREAD

Appleton Crewel Wool Yarn (www.purlsoho.com/purl/products/item/7449-Appleton-Crewel-Skeins).

Paternayan Persian Wool (http://sacoriverdyehouse.com/site).

Waverly Wool Needlepoint Yarn (http://brownsheep.com/yarns/waverly-wool).

ACID DYES AND TEXTILE PAINTS

Dharma Trading Company (www.dharmatrading.com).

Pro Chemical and Dye (www.prochemical.com).

Jacquard Products (www.jacquardproducts.com).

STAMPING SUPPLIES

Acrylic mounts for templates (www.stampin.com).

LAMP-MAKING SUPPLIES

The Lamp Shop (www.lampshop.com).

DIGITAL PRINTING ON DEMAND ON FABRIC

Spoonflower (www.spoonflower.com).

DOWN PILLOW INSERTS

OnlineFabricStore (www.onlinefabricstore.net).

WOOL FELT

A Child's Dream (www.achildsdream.com).
Purl Soho (www.purlsoho.com).
Weir Dolls and Crafts (www.weirdollsandcrafts.com).

SUNFLOWER SEEDS

Johnny's Selected Seeds (www.johnnyseeds.com).
Sunflower Selections (www.sunflowerselections.com).

ACKNOWLEDGMENTS

CREATING A HOUSE SUCH AS OURS IS A LABOR OF LOVE, creativity, and hard work. I have been fortunate to find talented people in my community who have helped turn my design dreams into a reality. First and foremost, Kevin Gray, my carpenter of almost thirty years, never says no to my wacky ideas and always finds a clever way to turn my sketches and ramblings into a finished space. Dave and Marsha LaPrade, my master electrician and his assistant, have rewired so many lamps and fixed so many problems—always with a smile and fun conversation. Will Pratt, our friend, real estate agent, and master patio builder, found the farmhouse for us and turned our hopes of owning an antique home and farm into a reality. Richard Rhodes, the former owner of Dakor Center and now the paint guru at Aubuchon Hardware in Greenfield, has taught me so much about which paint works for which project. Arthur Cohen turned my piles of antique metal parts into many lamps. My neighbor Debbie Bernard is always there with a smile and a helping hand when I am behind the eight ball with a deadline or a special event. Sid Herron has pulled me out of many a jam and is the best neighbor anyone could ever ask for.

I would be remiss if I didn't acknowledge the needleworkers, textile designers, fabric collectors, and flea market vendors of the past and from foreign lands who have made or sold to me the many fabrics I use in my home. Although I don't know their names, their spirit of creation and color and design plays a huge part in our colorful home and in my life. I also would like to thank the artists Matisse, Van Gogh, Bonnard, and the Fauve painters for experimenting with color and technique in the 1800s and bringing my favorite period of art to the world. To Vanessa Bell, Duncan Grant, and Roger Fry, thanks for bringing the creative spirit of the Bloomsbury Group to the interiors in their home, Charleston, East Sussex, which I find so inspiring, as do so many other textile artists.

I am so lucky that my friend Sally Lee invited us to her Maine island home many years ago. The wonderful friendship that began that rainy weekend, complete with a roaring fire on the Fourth of July, has been such a special one—full of textiles, art, color, fashion, flea markets, museums, and travel. Thank you for all you share.

I wouldn't have been able to complete the projects in this book without help from the following: My good friend Cathy Payson spent a weekend helping me sew the Crazy Quilt Swatch Blanket. Gail Callahan opened her dye studio and helped me dye pieces for the Crazy Quilt Swatch Blanket. Bonnie Reardon made the afghans.

Professionally, thanks go to Betsy Perry and Susan Mills of Classic Elite Yarns and Linda Pratt of Westminster Fibers for supporting my knitwear and authoring career with yarn and moral support. Ashley Spencer from Casart Coverings sells my dining room mural as removable wallpaper.

Thanks to Linda Roghaar, my literary agent, who encouraged me to turn our creatively decorated home into a book proposal and then found a home for it. Jennifer Urban-Brown, my editor at Roost Books, saw the potential of this project and has fashioned it into the book you hold in your hands. Thanks so much to Jenn, to assistant editor Julia Gaviria, to book designer Shubhani Sarkar, and to the entire team at Roost Books.

For the photos, I can't thank enough the talented Rikki Snyder, who sees my spaces and captures them in film as I see them in my head. Rikki—you are amazing. To Sarah Zimmerman—thanks so much for introducing yourself and Rikki while you were at Hallmark and for helping out on the long days of the shoot. To the readers of the Houzz.com website and to Rikki for writing and photographing the house for them—if you all hadn't responded so vocally and passionately, I wouldn't have thought to write this book.

Thanks to the readers and followers of my blog, *Getting Stitched on the Farm*—your comments and support continue to fuel my passions.

My mom, Nancy, inspired me as a young child as I watched her interior decoration forays come to life in our family home. Thanks, Mom, for all those lessons and discussions about color nuances that you probably don't remember nor thought I was paying attention to. Thanks, Dad, for going along with it all and for growing our garden and sharing your love of flowers, color, and raspberries. My incredible sisters—Lynn, Laurie, Nancy, and Jenn—and now their kids support my creative endeavors, even joining in with gusto. Thanks to the head cheerleader when I was a kid—my grandma Frieda Roessler Nicholas. If Gram could see where her stitching lessons have taken me, she would be over the moon.

Last, my husband, Mark Duprey, and our daughter, Julia Nicholas Duprey, are here every day putting up with the chaos and telling me my latest mess is beautiful. You two are the best. Love you both!

ABOUT THE AUTHOR

KRISTIN NICHOLAS GREW UP IN NORTHERN NEW JERSEY IN a creative family of five girls. Throughout her childhood, she sewed, quilted, crocheted, and embroidered. She studied textiles and clothing design at the University of Delaware, Oregon State University, and Colorado State University, where she taught herself to knit by hand. For sixteen years, she was creative director at Classic Elite Yarns. She has been designing for the knitting and needlework industry for over thirty years. Kristin is a knitting expert on PBS's *Knit and Crochet Now* and has appeared on *Martha Stewart TV* and many DIY television shows. She is the author of numerous books, including *Colorful Stitchery* (Roost Books, 2014).

Kristin met her farmboy husband, Mark Duprey, at Oregon State University. Together with their teenage daughter, Julia, they operate Leyden Glen Farm in western Massachusetts. The pasture-based sheep and lamb business focuses on supplying the local community with grass-fed lamb. Kristin writes the popular blog *Getting Stitched on the Farm*. You can see more of her work on her website, www.kristinnicholas.com.